Second Edition **Philosophy** through
CHRISTIANITY
for OCR B GCSE Religious Studies

Lorraine Abbott

HODDER
EDUCATION
AN HACHETTE UK COMPANY

Dedication

For Ellie, Lucy and Holly

  'Take the attitude of a student, never be too big to ask questions, never know too much to learn something new.'

Og Mendino (1923–1996)

Acknowledgement

David, Charles and Beeson, Hayley, Remy and Abi. Six great students to work with, a great source of encouragement and inspiration.

Exam advice, questions and hints revised and updated 2009 by Judith Anderson

The publishers would like to thank the following for permission to reproduce copyright material: Cover: *tl* akg-images, *tr* © Najlah Feanny/Corbis, *bl* Danita Delimont/Alamy, *br* © David Turnley/Corbis. Text: **p.9** *a* PROF. P. MOTTA/DEPT. OF ANATOMY/UNIVERSITY "LA SAPIENZA", ROME/SCIENCE PHOTO LIBRARY; **p.9** *b* VOLKER STEGER/SCIENCE PHOTO LIBRARY; **p.9** *c* SCOTT CAMAZINE/SCIENCE PHOTO LIBRARY; **p.9** *d* NHPA/John Shaw; **p.9** *e* SCOTT CAMAZINE/SCIENCE PHOTO LIBRARY; **p.9** *f* Nigel Cattlin/FLPA; **p.10** *l* front akg-images; **p.10** *l* back © NASA; **p.10** *r* front Mary Evans Picture Library; **p.10** *r* back © PBPA Paul Beard Photo Agency/Alamy; **p.11** *a* © George Diebold/Solus-Veer/Corbis; **p.11** *b* Getty Images/Sharon Montrose; **p.11** *c* Sipa Press/Rex Features; **p.13** © Muzeum Narodowe, Gdansk, Poland/The Bridgeman Art Library; **p.20** Rex Features; **p.22** © Look and Learn/The Bridgeman Art Library; **p.23** (tornado) © victor zastol'skiy/www.fotolia.com; **p.23** (fire) © klikk/www.fotolia.com; **p.29** © David L. Moore/Alamy; **p.30** *t* © ArkReligion.com/Alamy; **p.30** *b* © Tetra Images/Alamy; **p.31** Barry Batchelor/PA Archive/PA Photos; **p.32** © The Gallery Collection/Corbis; **p.33** *a* © Gonzalo Medina/www.istockphoto.com; **p.33** *b* © JOHN KOLESIDIS/Reuters/Corbis; **p.33** *c* British Red Cross; **p.34** *a* © Jenny Matthews/Alamy; **p.34** *b* Spencer Platt/Getty Images; **p.35** *c* © SW Productions/Brand X/Corbis; **p.35** *d* Christopher Furlong/Getty Images; **p.37** *a* © imagebroker/Alamy; **p.37** *b* © Scott Speakes/Corbis; **p.37** *c* © CLEO Photo/Alamy; **p.37** *d* © imagebroker/Alamy; **p.37** *e* © Macduff Everton/CORBIS; **p.38** *t* © The Photolibrary Wales/Alamy; **p.40** *t* © Christie's Images/CORBIS; **p.40** *b* © Johnathan Smith; Cordaiy Photo Library Ltd./CORBIS; **p.41** *a* © Paul Thompson Images/Alamy; **p.41** *b* © Albright-Knox Art Gallery/CORBIS; **p.41** *c* ARK Religion/Helene Rogers; **p.41** *d* © Spencer Williams; **p.42** © Wintershall Estate/www.wintershall-estate.com; **p.43** ABC Medya Ajansi/Rex Features; **p.45** © 24-7 Prayer; **p.46** *a* Last Resort Picture Library; **p.47** *b* Last Resort Picture Library; **p.47** *c* Last Resort Picture Library; **p.52** *t* © Jon Hicks/CORBIS; **p.52** *b* The Art Archive/Museo Nazionale Romano Rome/Alfredo Dagli Orti; **p.54** © The Art Publishing Group; **p.59** © Bloomimage/Corbis; **p.61** MATT DUNHAM/AP/PA Photos; **p.63** (background) © Kevin Lang/Alamy; **p.66** *tl* PHOTOGRAPH BY CAMERA PRESS LONDON; **p.66** *bl* PHOTOGRAPH BY CAMERA PRESS LONDON; **p.66** *tr* © Reuters/CORBIS; **p.66** *br* PHOTOGRAPH BY DAVID MOIR/TSPL, CAMERA PRESS LONDON; **p.67** *t* © Reuters/CORBIS; **p.67** *bl* © Sally and Richard Greenhill/Alamy; **p.67** *br* © ArkReligion.com/Alamy; **p.73** akg-images; **p.75** *a* BERNHARD EDMAIER/SCIENCE PHOTO LIBRARY; **p.75** *b* GEMUNU AMARASINGHE/AP/PA Photos; **p.75** *c* EDDIE MULHOLLAND/Rex Features; **p.75** *d* RENDRA TRISNADI/AFP/Getty Images; **p.75** *e* Ben Cawthra/Rex Features; **p.75** *f* JIM COLLINS/AP/PA Photos; **p.77** Answers in Genesis/www.answersingenesis.org; **p.80** M.C. Escher's "Three Worlds" © 2009 The M.C. Escher Company-Holland. All rights reserved. www.mcescher.com; **p.84** Last Resort Picture Library; **p.89** *t* © Lawrence Steigrad Fine Arts, New York/The Bridgeman Art Library; **p.89** *b* © www.ainvaresart.com; **p.90** *a* © ProfphotoXL/www.fotolia.com; **p.90** *b* © Gail Johnson/www.fotolia.com; **p.90** *c* © Katie Denham/www.fotolia.com; **p.90** *d* © Bettmann/CORBIS; **p.90** *e* © BlueOrange Studio/www.fotolia.com; **p.90** *f* © Grzegorz Kwolek/www.fotolia.com; **p.90** *g* © Marta/www.fotolia.com; **p.92** *a* © innershadows/www.fotolia.com; **p.92** *b* © Marek Kosmal/www.fotolia.com; **p.92** *c* © sciencephotos/Alamy; **p.92** © Gospel Communications International, Inc./www.reverendfun.com; **p.94** *t* © Museum of History and Industry/CORBIS; **p.94** *m* © Fred de Noyelle/Godong/Corbis; **p.94** *b* Sipa Press/Rex Features; **p.96** *a* © Matthew Polak/Sygma/Corbis; **p.96** *b* © Kristy-Anne Glubish/Design Pics/Corbis; **p.103** *a* Getty Images/Chip Simons; **p.103** *b* ADAM HART-DAVIS/SCIENCE PHOTO LIBRARY; **p.103** *c* © PBPA Paul Beard Photo Agency/Alamy; **p.104** SCIENCE PHOTO LIBRARY; **p.107** © Leonard de Selva/CORBIS; **p.108** © 2004 TopFoto/UPP; **p.111** © Pirate!/www.fotolia.com; **p.112** *b* Rex Features; **p.112** *c* © The Fairtrade Foundation; **p.112** *d* Richard Austin/Rex Features; **p.112** *e* This image is reproduced with kind permission of the Carbon Trust, and retains crown copyright ©2008; **p.113** *l & r* With acknowledgements to A Rocha International, Registered Charity #288634. For more information see www.arocha.org; **p.114** © Church Times. **The publishers would like to acknowledge use of the following extracts:** All Bible quotes are taken from the New International Version (NIV), published by Hodder & Stoughton Religious; **p.10** Dialogues concerning *Natural Religion* by David Hume, Oxford Paperbacks, 1998; **p.14** Continuum International Publishing Group for an extract from *The Catechism of the Catholic Church*, 2002; **p.20** http://news.bbc.co.uk/1/hi/magazine/4902332.stm; **p.29** 'At your feet we fall' by Dave Fellingham © 1982, Thankyou Music. Adm. by worshiptogether.com songs excl. UK & Europe, adm. by kingswaysongs, tym@kingsway.co.uk; **p.47** 'Love Life Live Lent' from www.cofe.anglican.org/news/pro607.html, quote from Right Rev David Urquhart, *Church Times*, 26 January 2007; **p.53** *Harry Potter and the Philosopher's Stone* by J. K. Rowling, Bloomsbury, 1997; **p.58** Information about purgatory from www.catholicchurch.org/faith/foundations/purgatory.htm **p.58** (left) G.K. Chesterton, *Orthodoxy*, 1908 **p.58** (right) Continuum International Publishing Group for an extract from *The Catechism of the Catholic Church*, 2002; **p.61** http://news.sky.com, 4 March 2006; **p.71** *The Screwtape Letters* by C.S. Lewis, Fount, 1998; **p.72** Continuum International Publishing Group for an extract from *The Catechism of the Catholic Church*, 2002; **p.76** www.newadvent.org/cathen/05649a.htm; **p.93** *Mere Christianity* by C.S. Lewis, Fount, 1997; **p.101** Stephen Hawking quoted in *Der Spiegel*, 1989; **p.102** Stephen Hawking quoted in the *Guardian*, 27 September 2005; **p.108** www.counterbalance.net/transcript/ssq2-body.html; **p.111** 'Iranians buy Soviet 'killer' dolphins', by Richard Beeston, *The Times*, 10 March 2000. **Every effort has been made to trace all copyright holders, but if any have been inadvertently overlooked the Publishers will be pleased to make the necessary arrangements at the first opportunity.**

Although every effort has been made to ensure that website addresses are correct at time of going to press, Hodder Education cannot be held responsible for the content of any website mentioned in this book. It is sometimes possible to find a relocated web page by typing in the address of the home page for a website in the URL window of your browser.

Hachette UK's policy is to use papers that are natural, renewable and recyclable products and made from wood grown in sustainable forests. The logging and manufacturing processes are expected to conform to the environmental regulations of the country of origin.

Orders: please contact Bookpoint Ltd, 130 Milton Park, Abingdon, Oxon OX14 4SB. Telephone: +44 (0)1235 827720. Fax: +44 (0)1235 400454. Lines are open 9.00–5.00, Monday to Saturday, with a 24-hour message answering service. Visit our website at www.hoddereducation.co.uk.

© Lorraine Abbott 2009
First published in 2009 by
Hodder Education,
An Hachette UK company
338 Euston Road
London NW1 3BH

Impression number   5   4   3
Year   2013   2012   2211   2010

Illustrations by Clive Spong at Linden Artists and Oxford Designers and Illustrators
Typeset in Gill Sans Light 10.5pt and produced by Gray Publishing, Tunbridge Wells, Kent
Printed in Italy

A catalogue record for this title is available from the British Library
ISBN 978 0 340 98411 6

Contents

Introduction

This book has been written specifically to support the philosophy topics of the OCR Religious Studies B (Philosophy and Applied Ethics) GCSE course. The book is divided into the following six philosophy topics and looks at them from a Christian perspective:

- Topic 1 The Nature of God
- Topic 2 Religious and Spiritual Experience
- Topic 3 The End of Life

Unit B601

- Topic 4 Good and Evil
- Topic 5 Religion, Reason and Revelation
- Topic 6 Religion and Science

Unit B602

Each topic starts by outlining the key concepts that you will need to learn about in order to answer examination questions successfully.

About the exam

Each Unit is worth 25 per cent of the total GCSE marks (unless you are doing the short course and then each Unit is worth 50 per cent of the marks). The exam paper for each Unit is one hour long and contains a question on each of the three different topic areas within it. You will need to choose and then answer two questions from the three. Each question is worth 24 marks so in total there will be 48 marks on each paper/unit. Each question is divided into five parts – you will need to attempt all the parts: (a), (b), (c), (d) and (e).

The exam questions aim to assess your level of knowledge and understanding of the material as well as your capabilities to analyse and evaluate different beliefs and attitudes. In order to achieve maximum marks, it is useful for you to be aware of what is generally expected for each type of question.

Question a)

This part of the question is worth one mark and your answer should show your knowledge and understanding of a concept. So, for instance, you might be asked 'What is prayer?' and your answer should show that you know what 'prayer' means.

Question b)

This part of the question is worth two marks and asks for two ideas within a concept. So, for instance, you might be asked what is meant by the term 'soul' and you would respond by giving two ideas about the soul.

Question c)

This part of the question is worth three marks and asks for three ideas within a concept. So, for instance, you might be asked to describe how Christians worship and you would need to give three different ideas as to what they do in worship.

Question d)

This part of the question is worth six marks and asks you to describe and explain a belief or attitude, while analysing the reasons Christians respond in this way. So, for instance, you might be asked to explain Christian beliefs about miracles or why Christians believe there is a God. You could try to include relevant Christian teachings to support the ideas you are giving. If you use a biblical quote, you must make sure you explain what the quote means in order to show the examiner that you have understood what the quote is saying. For instance, God told Adam and Eve to 'go forth and multiply' (Genesis 1: 28) – this means to 'go and have children'. You will also need to use specific religious words in these answers when they are relevant. For example, when answering a question on how God created human beings you may like to refer to the term *imago dei*, which means 'in the image of God'. This term shows that human beings were created by God and so are special.

Question e)

This part of the question is worth 12 marks and asks you to show different points of view in response to the statement given. So, for instance, you might be given the statement 'If God existed we would know it' and you would need to refer to a Christian point of view, showing that there are different Christian theories of why God exists and perhaps contrast these views with an atheist or scientific point of view. Then you will need to give your own personal response. Try to make that response different, if you can, to the ones you have mentioned previously. It is very important that you do give your own point of view otherwise you will not achieve high marks. You will need to support the Christian ideas with reference to Christian teachings/biblical quotes. Again, make sure you explain them in your own words to show your understanding.

Make sure you answer what the question is asking. Many candidates do not achieve the grade they hoped to get because they failed to do this. For instance, if the question is asking you to discuss Christian ideas on the origins of humanity make sure you stay focused on how God created Adam and Eve and do not get sidetracked into discussing in detail the different stages/days on how God created everything else, such as when the stars and moon were created.

Trigger words

The exam questions may ask for you to respond to various trigger words:

Attitudes	Are the ways in which a Christian might interpret their beliefs. This trigger word means that there are different Christian approaches and you should try to show that there are different ways in which a Christian might respond.
Beliefs	What Christians believe in/their faith.
Describe	This word is asking you to give information about something. Try not to just make a list of ideas but show that you have lots of knowledge about an idea.
Explain	This word is asking you to say why something happens so you should use the word 'because'.
Respond	This word is asking you to show how and why a Christian would act.
Teachings	These are quotes/sayings/rules from the Bible or Church authorities.

About the book

Throughout the book you will find the following features.

Key Concepts

At the start of every topic there is a short section called Key Concepts, which outlines the main ideas that you will learn about in the topic.

TASK

The tasks help you to record information, respond to Christian beliefs and develop your written communication in preparation for the exam. The tasks are varied and challenging.

To discuss

Philosophical topics raise ultimate questions. For many people there are no clear-cut answers to such questions and for this reason it is important for you to spend time discussing them with others. This feature encourages you to do this. Developing an understanding of others' views will help you to answer the part (e) questions on the exam paper.

STRETCH WHAT YOU KNOW

It is always good to extend your learning by using a variety of resources, for example the internet, or by engaging in more challenging tasks. To support the extension of your learning there are a number of these 'stretching tasks' throughout the book.

EXAM FOCUS ...

There are exam-style questions throughout the book to give you practice in answering different types of exam questions.

... HINTS

This feature gives you guidance on what to include in your exam answers and how to structure them.

 **Bible bitz**

You don't have to learn lots of quotes for your exam, but in order to explain Christian attitudes, teachings and beliefs you need to know what they are based on. The Bible bitz give you some biblical teachings to support your knowledge and understanding.

 **Link it up**

The ability to link beliefs to behaviour is a skill needed when answering some parts of the examination questions. This feature gives you the opportunity to practise this skill.

IN THE NEWS

The philosophical issues that you are studying are relevant in our society today, so much so that you can sometimes hear about them in the news. This feature helps you to consider philosophical issues in relation to current events.

Lorraine

This feature contains real views from real people with a Christian faith. The views that you read in this feature show how the beliefs and attitudes that you learn about can be applied in society today.

The Nature of God

Key Concepts

In this topic you will learn about:

- Philosophical arguments for the existence of God
- Christian beliefs about the nature of God
- Reasons Christians give in support of their belief in God
- Belief in God intervening in the world through MIRACLES
- Belief in God intervening in the world through Jesus.
- Belief in God intervening in the world through the Holy Spirit.

Christians are monotheists – they believe that there is only one God. However, they believe that God can be known and has revealed himself in three different ways, as Father, Son and Holy Spirit. This belief is known as the DOCTRINE of the TRINITY. Christians have many reasons for their belief in God, including evidence from the Bible, the sense of right and wrong that human beings have, and their own personal experiences of God. Christians believe that God continues to be involved in the world and evidence of this may be seen in his intervention through miracles, the person of Christ and the Holy Spirit.

A matter of belief

People's beliefs are based on what they consider to be reliable evidence, and this applies to people's beliefs about the existence of God. Often, visible evidence is considered the most reliable source of evidence. For example, people will claim belief in something because they have 'seen it with their own eyes'. However, people usually consider a range of evidence to arrive at their beliefs.

Complete the task below to help you to identify what evidence you choose to rely on for some of your own beliefs.

TASKS

Real

1 Draw out and label a line as shown.

2 Place each item from the list below somewhere along the line, based on your level of belief in their existence.

- Fairies
- Wind
- Jesus
- Father Christmas
- Ghosts
- Inuit
- God
- Satan

3 What criteria did you use to determine your level of belief for each of the things on the list? For example, does having visual evidence for its existence put it higher up your list?

4 Compare your work with the rest of your class. Explain why there are differences in people's beliefs.

Fictional

Philosophical arguments for the existence of God

In philosophy there are reasoned arguments, based on evidence, which try to prove the existence of God.

Two of the main arguments are:

■ the teleological argument
■ the cosmological argument.

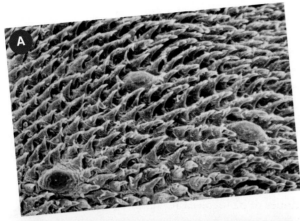

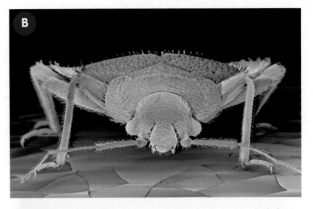

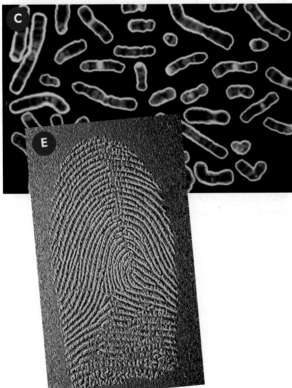

To discuss

1 Try to identify what each of the images A–F shows.

2 What conclusions might you draw about the natural world from this collection of images? For example, would any of the images lead you to agree with the points on the right:

■ The natural world contains a great deal of beauty.
■ The world is intricate.
■ The world has been carefully designed.
■ Every person is unique.

3 What other images would you add to these six to reflect your conclusions?

TASK

Read Hume's and Paley's accounts of the teleological argument and then:

■ explain the argument in your own words
■ list any problems that you can see with this argument.

The six images on page 9 show different aspects of the natural world:

A = magnified image of human tongue
B = magnified image of bed bug
C = strands of DNA
D = detail of a leaf
E = human fingerprint
F = centre of a flower

Some PHILOSOPHERS have suggested that observation of the natural world reveals an order and complexity that can only have been achieved through intelligent design. This means that instead of coming into existence through a chain of natural events, the world is the result of a design by an intelligent being – God. This argument for the existence of God is known as the teleological argument. It takes its name from the Greek word *telos*, meaning 'purpose', and suggests that because the world was designed it has a purpose. This argument is also known as the argument from design.

David Hume
*Philosopher
1711–76*

'**Look around the world: Contemplate [think about] the whole and every part of it: You will find it to be nothing but one great machine, subdivided into an infinite number of lesser machines … All these various machines and even their minute parts, are adjusted to each other with an accuracy … the Author [designer] of Nature is somewhat similar to the mind of man, though possessed [having] of much larger faculties, due to the grandeur of the work which he has executed. By this argument … do we prove at once the existence of a Deity [God] and his similarity to human mind and intelligence.**'

From **Dialogues concerning Natural Religion**, *1776*

William Paley
*Philosopher
1743–1805*

Paley uses the example of a watch to explain the argument. He said that the way in which all the parts of a watch work together to meet a purpose suggest that the watch must have a designer. This is because such order and purpose could not be assumed to be simply the result of an accident. He said that, in the same way, if you look at the world and the way nature appears to work to meet a purpose, it also suggests that the world must have a designer – God.

The cosmological argument

Another philosophical argument for the existence of God is the cosmological argument. It is called the cosmological argument because it tries to INFER the existence of God from the existence of the COSMOS or universe and the events within it.

> ### To discuss
>
> **4** Look at the pictures below and what is happening in each. Discuss what the cause(s) for each event may be.
>
> **5** Is it possible for something to happen that has no cause?

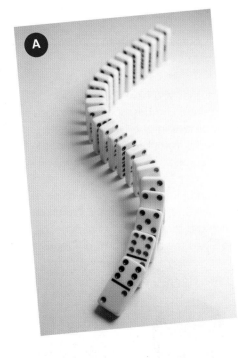

A

B

C

STRETCH WHAT YOU KNOW

Thomas Aquinas' arguments for the existence of God are often referred to as the Five Ways:

1 The Unmoved Mover.

2 The Uncaused Causer.

3 Possibility and Necessity.

4 Goodness, Truth and Nobility.

5 Teleological:

- Using www.newadvent.org/summa/1002.htm#article3, follow the link to the existence of God.

- Find out what is meant by the second and third of Aquinas' arguments.

- Summarise the two arguments in two clear written paragraphs.

There is, in fact, no event in the natural world that is without a cause. This idea was identified by the philosopher Plato (428–348BCE), who said that every created thing must be created by some cause. The cosmological argument suggests, therefore, that the universe must have a cause, since something must have triggered off the process that started the development of the universe – rather like someone pushing over the first domino in a line and then observing the rest falling down. In this argument, God is this prime mover, or first cause. God himself is without cause. One philosopher who developed this argument was Thomas Aquinas (1225–74).

Both the teleological and the cosmological arguments for the existence of God rely on reasoning to try to prove their case. Christians may accept one or both of these arguments, but their belief in the existence of God is also based on further evidence and argument.

> ### To discuss
>
> **6** What other reasons do you think Christians might give for their belief in the existence of God?

The Nature of God 11

Christian beliefs about the nature of God

TASKS

1 Create a SYMBOL or small picture to illustrate each of the characteristics of God listed on the right. For example, you could draw a halo to represent perfection, or a judge's hammer to represent the idea of a judge. Combine all of these images on to one page to make a poster.

2 Now look at your poster without the list in front of you. How many of the characteristics of God can you identify? Write a short paragraph describing the character of God based on your poster.

To discuss

1 What role is the woman taking on in each of the three pictures on this page?

2 How could these pictures be used to help explain the Christian idea of the Trinity?

3 Develop another ANALOGY to help explain the Christian idea of the Trinity. An analogy is using one idea to illustrate or explain another. Another example is the shamrock below.

Christians do not believe in a God who is limited by the LAWS OF NATURE or by a physical body. They believe that God has certain unique characteristics that make him holy. To Christians God is:

- omnipotent – all powerful
- omniscient – all knowing
- omnipresent – able to be everywhere at once because he is not limited by a physical body
- ETERNAL – without a beginning or an end, outside of time and space
- perfectly good
- our judge.

God can be described using his characteristics, as you have done in your poster in the task, but Christians also understand and describe God through the way he has revealed himself. Christians believe in one God, but they believe that their one God has revealed himself as three separate persons. This belief in one God revealed through three persons is known as the Trinity.

Each person in the Trinity – Father, Son and Holy Spirit – fulfils a different role. The Father is often referred to simply as God, and the Son is identified by Christians as Jesus. Both God the Father and the Holy Spirit are unseen, while Christians believe that Jesus, the Son, was the human form of God who lived on earth over 2000 years ago and then returned to heaven after his RESURRECTION. All three persons of the Trinity are eternal.

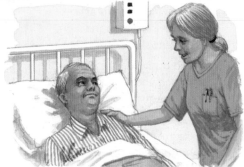

A shamrock has one stem but three leaves. This is what the Trinity is like.

... the Lord
... Is he not your Father, your Creator,
who made you and formed you?

Deuteronomy 32: 6

... let your light shine before men, that they
may see your good deeds and praise your
Father in heaven.

Matthew 5: 16

Grace and peace from God the Father and
Christ Jesus our Saviour.

Titus 1: 4

In the presence of God and of Christ Jesus, who
will judge the living and the dead ...

2 Timothy 4: 1

Jesus Christ ... is the ATONING SACRIFICE for our
SINS ... for the sins of the whole world.

1 John 2: 2

Your attitude should be the same as that of
Christ Jesus:
Who, being in very nature God ...
Taking the very nature of a servant,
being made in human likeness ...

Philippians 2: 6

... the Counsellor, the Holy Spirit, whom the
Father will send in my name, will teach you all
things and will remind you of everything I
[Jesus] have said to you.

John 14: 26

... the Spirit of him who raised Jesus from the
dead is living in you ...

Romans 8: 11

The Holy Spirit with a Model of Ptolemy's World by Hermann Han, 1610.

Link it up

1 List all you can about the nature of the
Father, Son and Holy Spirit under three
headings based on the information in the
Bible quotes. For example:

Father
He is in heaven   (Matthew 5: 16)

2 Read the section on Christian beliefs on
pages 14–15 and add any additional
information about the nature of the Father,
Son and Holy Spirit to your lists.

TASKS

Look at Han's painting, which portrays all three
members of the Trinity

3 Who is represented by:
   ■ the dove
   ■ the white-bearded man
   ■ the second bearded man?
   What makes you identify each figure in this way?

4 What do you think the Trinity are doing in this
painting of them?

5 Explain whether you think this image is helpful in
understanding the idea of the Trinity.

God the Father

Christians believe that God the Father is the Creator. This is expressed in the APOSTLES' CREED in the Church of England's Alternative Service Book:

> I believe in God, the Father almighty,
> creator of heaven and earth.

In the Bible Christians are taught to speak to God using the phrase 'Abba, Father' (Romans 8: 15). Abba may be understood as similar to calling God 'daddy' – a way of showing the close, loving relationship that Christians may have with the creator.

God as Father also conveys a sense of safety and protection for those who are his followers. This can be seen in Proverbs 18: 10 where the righteous are said to be safe in God's strength.

God the Son

Jesus is believed to be God INCARNATED. In the Apostles' Creed it says:

> I believe in Jesus Christ, God's only Son, our
> Lord, who was conceived by the Holy Spirit,
> born of the Virgin Mary …

This means that to Christians Jesus is God taking on flesh and appearing on earth in a human form. Christians believe that Jesus was not conceived naturally but placed in Mary by the Holy Spirit. They believe that because Jesus was not made by two humans, he was free of all SIN, unlike all other humans. Although the idea is a very difficult one, Jesus is understood to be completely human but also completely God. God came to earth in the form of Jesus for three main purposes:

1 To reveal God to people, showing his love and power and teaching them how he wants people to live.
2 To sacrifice himself on the cross, receiving God's punishment for human sin in order for REPENTANT people to be forgiven.
3 To rise from the dead to show that God has power over death, that he is eternal, and that Christians, too, may have an everlasting life in heaven after death.

God the Holy Spirit

In the Bible the Spirit of God is often referred to using the Greek word *Paraclete*. The word *paraclete* means 'one who comes alongside someone else'. The Spirit is therefore understood as the one who is with Christians as their constant guide and comforter. His presence in the lives of believers is described in the Bible in Acts 2:4 when he comes at PENTECOST:

> All of them were filled with the Holy Spirit and began to speak in other tongues as the Spirit enabled them.

Christians believe that the Spirit helps them to live in the way God requires, helping them to understand his teaching and giving them the promise of life with him in heaven after death.

The mystery of the Most Holy Trinity is the central mystery of the Christian faith and of Christian life. God alone can make it known to us by revealing himself as Father, Son and Holy Spirit.

The Catechism of the Catholic Church, 261

STRETCH WHAT YOU KNOW

1 What does the Catechism of the Catholic Church identify as the central mystery of Christianity?

2 How can this mystery be made known to humans?

3 Why do you think the Catechism refers to the Trinity as a mystery? Do you agree?

Lorraine

The Holy Spirit is probably the part of the Trinity that I have the closest sense of because I believe that as a Christian he is always with me in some way. The best way of explaining this is to think of him as a constant friend always there to encourage or support me. Obviously I can't see him, rather I sense his presence. I can think of times in my life where everything seemed to be going wrong, where a situation couldn't have turned out worse and yet I have felt the Holy Spirit giving me a feeling of peace, helping me to know that God will work through the situation.

I was once told the story of an artist who entered a painting of a storm into a competition to produce a picture of calm. The artist was asked how on earth his stormy picture showed calm. The artist then pointed to a nest in the trees in which a bird was sitting on her eggs, unmoved by the chaos around her. This to me reflects the effect of the Holy Spirit in my life, always there, a 'paraclete' despite the chaos that may be going on in my life. I am encouraged in my faith to know that Jesus has promised that the Holy Spirit will never leave me or let me down.

To discuss

4 Lorraine says that although she cannot see the Holy Spirit she can sense his presence. In the natural world we cannot see the wind but we certainly know it is there when it blows through the trees. Can you think of any other examples from the natural world of things we cannot see but we know exist?

5 Can you identify a time in your life when you have acted as a *paraclete* to someone else?

6 What is the difference between you acting as a *paraclete* at different times in your life and Lorraine's description of the Holy Spirit as a *paraclete*?

EXAM FOCUS ...

Describe the Christian beliefs about the nature of God.

question d), 6 marks

... HINTS

■ This question is asking you to describe what Christians think about God and what he does so do not get sidetracked in trying to say why Christians believe in God.

■ You could begin your answer by stating that Christians believe in one God who has many roles or characteristics and then go on to describe what God does.

■ You could support your statements by referring to the Bible bitz on page 13. However, do not just put them in your answer, instead make sure you use them to support your statements about what God is like or what God does.

Reasons Christians give in support of their belief in God

A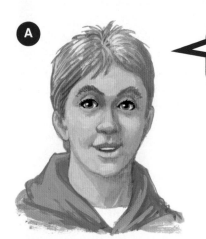

I believe God exists because someone must have caused the universe to come into existence. Everything has a cause. The universe is so massive that I believe God must be its cause.

B

Have you ever stopped to look at the world we live in? It is so beautiful and complex, I don't think this all happened accidentally. I believe that it was planned and created. Nature itself gives me reason to believe that God exists.

C

I believe that God answers PRAYERS. This doesn't mean we always get what we pray for, but that God will do what is best for us in the situations that we pray about. Answers to prayer are my reason for believing in God.

D

In the Bible Jesus performed miracles and even today miracles are happening around the world. I believe God does exist and is still being experienced by people today through miracles.

E

To me God must exist because I have a real sense of right and wrong – a conscience – and I think this has been given by God.

F

Ever since I was little I have been taught that God exists. I can't see any reason not to believe this and my religion forms a very important part of my life.

And the Lord God said, 'The man has now become like one of us, knowing good and evil.'

Genesis 3: 22

In the beginning God created the heavens and the earth.

Genesis 1: 1

For by him [Christ] all things were created: things in heaven and on earth, visible and invisible ... all things were created by him and for him.

Colossians 1: 16

Then you will call upon me and come and pray to me, and I will listen to you.

Jeremiah 29: 12

Every word of God is flawless.

Proverbs 30: 5

By the power of signs and miracles ... I have fully proclaimed the GOSPEL of Christ.

Romans 15:19

I don't know if God exists, but it would be better for His reputation if He didn't.

Jules Renard, French writer (1864–1910)

The Bible tells people that God exists and it explains who he is and how people can get to know him. I believe the Bible is proof that God is real.

TASKS

1 Read each of the viewpoints on pages 16–17.
2 Divide a piece of paper into three columns as shown below:

Reasons Christians may give for God's existence	Bible quotes	Arguments against this view

3 In the left-hand column summarise the arguments given in each of the speech bubbles.
4 In the middle column write down any supporting evidence from the Bible quotes on the left.
5 In the right-hand column write down arguments against each of the Christian views. You may find it helpful to discuss this in pairs before filling the column in. You could use the arguments listed below to help trigger your discussions and start by matching these to the Christian view they argue against:

a Not everyone has the same sense of right and wrong, for example ...
b Prayers only appear to be answered because of coincidences ...
c There is so much that goes wrong in our natural world. For example ...
d The Bible is written by people who may have believed what they wrote but they were wrong.
e Just because occasionally someone gets well against all the odds does not mean that a miracle has happened.
f Our universe was caused by a big explosion – it was a completely natural process.
g We should question the things we are taught – just because someone tells you something is true does not mean that it is.

To discuss

Jules Renard refers to God's reputation. When he said this he was thinking of the negative ideas people have of God.

1 How do we know Renard was thinking of the negative ideas that people have of God?
2 What negative ideas of God do people have?
3 Do the ideas that you have come up with make it more or less likely for you to believe in God?

Jo

I became a Christian four years ago at the age of 25. I had always been fascinated that some people had this belief in a power outside of this world, yet I had never been to church.

I first went to church in June 2003 when my boyfriend (now my husband of two and a half years) invited me to his church in Plymouth. It was all very new to me and I thought it would just be similar to the few services I had been to at other churches – sing songs, hear someone speak at the front for ten minutes and probably be a bit bored! It was nothing like that at all! I remember watching people PRAISING and worshipping God and, although I didn't understand it at that point, I remember thinking 'There's something special and different about these people'. Something I wanted to have but I didn't know what it was. They had a real freedom and a certainty and confidence in what they believed.

I had to keep going back to understand more about the beliefs of the people I met at the church. It was three or four months later that I actually made the decision to become a Christian. The only thing I knew is that something had changed in me. I had a good life, good job, great family but I knew that inside there was something missing – I knew I was empty. I knew I couldn't walk away from this, although at that point I still didn't totally understand everything about Christianity. Knowing the truth had set me free!

When I made that decision, not only was I free from the grasp of the devil on my life but Jesus also freed me from other vices I had in my life. Within the first six months of becoming a Christian, Jesus healed me from a mild form of the eating disorder bulimia. I had always had problems with my weight fluctuating and had previously suffered depression through issues with food. The truth of Jesus giving his life for me set me free from my past and now I don't have a problem with food. I am a new creation in Jesus Christ! It's exciting and I'm looking forward to the good plan God has for the rest of my life!

TASKS

6 How does Jo describe her life as a Christian?

7 What reasons does Jo give for becoming a Christian?

8 In what way does Jo believe that her FAITH in God has helped her?

9 What questions would you ask Jo about her faith in God if you were able to?

EXAM FOCUS ...

'God cannot be seen and there is no evidence that he exists.'

Discuss this statement. You should include different, supported points of view and a personal viewpoint. You must refer to Christianity in your answer.

question e), 12 marks

... HINTS

- Remember – it is important to show different points of view and also your own personal point of view.
- This question is asking you to discuss and evaluate (look at the arguments for and against) and then come to a conclusion on whether the statement is true or false. You may not want to agree or disagree entirely – that is fine but you must support your conclusion with a valid reason.
- You could start by giving a Christian response either by using some of the arguments on pages 16–18 or by using some of the theological proofs – cosmological or design arguments – as a way of disagreeing with the statement.
- You may wish to refer to the fact that no one in the Bible sees God and that in Exodus 33: 20 God tells Moses 'you cannot see my face, for no one may see me and live'.
- Then you could give a secular view as to why some people might say that God does not exist in order to agree with the statement.
- Then remember to give your own personal view.

Belief in God intervening in the world through miracles

Christians believe that God intervened in the world when he sent his son Jesus to earth. Many Christians believe that God still intervenes today through miraculous works. A miracle may be defined as a SUPERNATURAL event or act. Christians understand this to be when God intervenes and apparently overrules the LAWS OF NATURE. For example, if Christians pray for a person who has been blind since birth and the person's sight returns, that could be regarded as a miracle.

Miracles can be divided into four main categories:

- healing miracles – when someone who is unwell immediately returns to health, or when a person who has been told by doctors that they are dying from an incurable disease actually recovers
- miracles over nature – when the natural elements are controlled, for example, when a storm suddenly ceases
- raising the dead miracles – when someone who is declared dead returns to life
- exorcisms – when a person who is believed to be possessed by an evil spirit has that evil spirit sent out of their body.

Many Christians believe that God can and does still intervene in the world today through miracles. For example, over 6500 people claimed to have been miraculously healed at Lourdes, a town in southern France, although the Catholic Church has only officially recognised 67 healing miracles there. Lourdes became a place of Christian pilgrimage in 1858 after Bernadette Soubirous, a fourteen-year-old girl, claimed to have experienced eighteen separate visions of the Virgin Mary. On 9 November 2005, the Catholic Church declared Anna Santaniello, an Italian, to be the sixty-seventh person to have been miraculously cured at Lourdes, 53 years after her healing experience. On 19 August 1952, at the age of 41, she was cured after being bathed in the water of Lourdes while on a pilgrimage. Prior to her healing she had several illnesses including severe heart disease and excessive breathlessness (Bouillaud's disease), which made it impossible for her to walk and very difficult for her to speak. When the medical committee based at Lourdes and the Catholic Church reviewed her case in 2005, she was 93 years old and still in good health. The Catholic Church never rushes to make quick judgements in these cases and is always careful to authenticate the miracle claims that are made.

Some Christian ministries believe that God is working through them to bring about miracles in the world today. For example, evangelist Benny Hinn holds healing services around the world and he claims to have held the largest ever healing service during a mission in India. He says 'His [God's] ability to perform the miraculous is not and never has been restricted to a certain time frame in Church history … Miracles still happen! And they are available to you and me!'

While Christians may disagree on the authenticity of individual or specific miracles they largely agree that God is able to perform miracles today just as he did in the biblical accounts.

TASKS

1 Do you think the possibility that God performed miracles in biblical times makes it more or less likely that he performs miracles today? Consider what Benny Hinn says as you answer this question.
2 Why do you think the Catholic Church is so careful about officially recognising miracles?
3 How credible do you believe the case of Anna Santaniello to be? You can read more about it at www.lourdes-france.org (click on the Union flag to get the English version).

EXAM FOCUS …

Explain Christian beliefs about miracles.

question d), 6 marks

… HINTS

- You could begin by stating what a miracle is, and then refer to an example of a miracle either from the Bible or from a modern-day example or both.
- Remember – Christians have different ideas about the miracles in the Bible; some believe they happened exactly as the Bible says while others believe the miracles are symbolic and they contain a message on how Christians should act or show God's power (the Gospel of John refers to miracles as 'signs'). For example, the feeding of the 5000 contains the message to help others.
- You could refer to how Christians show their belief in miracles through prayer and by making pilgrimages to places such as Lourdes.

Raj Persaud's account of his trip to Lourdes

Making a radio programme about one of the most remarkable places on earth – Lourdes – was always going to be demanding and precarious.

This is because Lourdes as a place where miracles occur and PILGRIMS are cured of serious diseases has a very special place in the hearts of the religious.

Now, millions from all around the world visit this eerie place. I am primarily a scientist and a doctor, and of course science strives constantly to be objective, not subjective. So I wanted to make a scientific investigation of whether miracles really happen – or is there some other more mundane explanation for the mysterious phenomena of Lourdes?

What I found, much to my surprise, is that it seems even hard-headed scientists can still be convinced in the twenty-first century that miracles, which violate the known laws of nature, still happen.

But perhaps most intriguing of all was encountering, as we did in the programme, a man who appeared to have been cured of multiple sclerosis during an astonishing visit to

Lourdes, and whose cure was ratified by the doctors and scientists as scientifically inexplicable.

This man, although largely serene, did seem a little troubled now by the ultimate question, which was: 'Given many go to Lourdes and don't receive the blessing of a cure, why was he singled out for a miracle?'

It seems that even for those who believe in miracle cures or have directly experienced them there remains this last disquieting question – why me?

Dr Raj Persaud MSc MPhil MRCPsych
Consultant Psychiatrist

 ## Link it up

1 Identify which category each of the miracles in the pictures and Bible quotes on page 21 falls into:

   ■ healing miracle
   ■ nature miracle
   ■ raising the dead miracle.

2 What was shown by Jesus performing miracles, according to the writer of Acts (see artwork D)?

3 What do you think God's intervention in the world through miracles leads Christians to believe about God?

To discuss

Read the 'In the News' article above and discuss the following questions:

1 Do you think the article proves that miracles happen today?
2 What other explanations might there be for the man's recovery from multiple sclerosis?
3 If the man's recovery was a miraculous event caused by God, what questions would this lead you to ask about God?

STRETCH WHAT YOU KNOW

Go to www.aca.org.nz click on testimonials and select a healing miracle.

1 Summarise the account in your own words.

2 Identify any similarities with the biblical miracles described on page 21 or any other accounts of miracles in the Bible that you know.

3 Explain fully your own view of the apparent miracle. This might include further questions about the event to which you would like answers.

A man with leprosy came and knelt before him [Jesus] and said, 'Lord, if you are willing, you can make me clean.' Jesus reached out and touched the man ... Immediately he was cured of his leprosy.

Matthew 8: 2–3

A furious squall came up, and the waves broke over the boat, so that it was nearly swamped. Jesus was in the stern, sleeping ... The disciples woke him and said to him, 'Teacher, don't you care if we drown?' He got up, rebuked the wind and said to the waves, 'Quiet! Be still!' Then the wind died down and it was completely calm.

Mark 4: 37–39

As he [Jesus] approached the town gate, a dead person was being carried out – the only son of his mother, and she was a widow. And a large crowd from the town was with her. When the Lord saw her, his heart went out to her and he said, 'Don't cry.' Then he went up and touched the coffin ... He said, 'Young man, I say to you, get up!' The dead man sat up and began to talk, and Jesus gave him back to his mother.

Luke 7: 12–15

Men of Israel, listen to this: Jesus of Nazareth was a man accredited by God to you by miracles ... which God did among you through him.

Acts 2: 22

Belief in God intervening in the world through Jesus

For Christians the most significant way in which God has shown his involvement with the world is when he came to earth as Jesus. In the GOSPEL of John it says:

> The Word [Jesus] became flesh and made his dwelling among us. We have seen his glory, the glory of the One and Only, who came from the Father.
>
> *John 1: 14*

The extract reflects the Christian belief that God himself took on human form by coming to earth as Jesus. This was God's way of showing to other humans what he was like.

As a human Jesus was aware of the pressures, emotions and realities that all people experience. However, at the same time that he was fully human he was also fully God and thus he remained perfect in all ways. Christians believe that by coming to earth in this way God has shown his absolute love for the people that he created. This love was ultimately shown through Jesus' death and RESURRECTION:

> God demonstrates his own love for us in this: While we were still sinners, Christ died for us.
>
> *Romans 5: 8*

Christians come to know about Jesus through the Gospels. In the person of Jesus, God shows himself in a way that humans can understand. In this sense God has literally been seen in history and can still be seen through the biblical writings today.

Jesus Teaching, a twentieth-century book illustration. Many thousands of people heard Jesus' teaching during his three years of ministry. He didn't teach just through what he said but through his life, his miracles and his sacrificial death.

TASKS

1 What do you think makes a good teacher?

2 What indications are there in the Bible that suggest that Jesus was an effective teacher?

3 Why do you think God chose to use the incarnation the way to meet with people?

Belief in God intervening in the world through the Holy Spirit

Christians believe that the Holy Spirit is permanently within each and every Christian. He is a gift from God sent by Jesus after his ASCENSION. In this way God's intervention in the world is ongoing and personal.

The coming of the Holy Spirit at Pentecost

Before Jesus ascended he told his disciples that by leaving them to return to be with his Father in heaven he would be able to send the Holy Spirit, also described as the comforter, to be with them. In Acts, Luke records that the apostles were told by Jesus to remain in Jerusalem until they had received the Holy Spirit. It was the power that they received from him that was to help them to be witnesses throughout the world. Acts records the arrival of the Holy Spirit at PENTECOST.

Suddenly a sound like the blowing of a violent wind came from heaven and filled the whole house where they were sitting. They saw what seemed to be tongues of fire that separated and came to rest on each of them. All of them were filled with the Holy Spirit and began to speak in other tongues as the Spirit enabled them (Acts 2: 2–4).

TASK

The description in Acts 2 of the coming of the Holy Spirit is often believed to be symbolic. What characteristics of wind and fire do you think the writer of Acts wanted his readers to apply to the character of the Holy Spirit?

Describing The Holy Spirit as a 'violent wind' reflects the power of the Spirit while the tongues of fire suggest the warmth and purity of the Spirit. The result of the coming of the Holy Spirit is then seen throughout the book of Acts and the rest of the Bible as the apostles proclaim the message of Jesus fearlessly. The apostles are transformed from a scared group of men after Jesus' death and RESURRECTION to bold individuals declaring the deity of Jesus to all who will listen. There are accounts of people becoming Christians and often large numbers of people at a time are converted.

Evidence of the Holy Spirit in the lives of believers

The evidence of the presence of the Holy Spirit within a Christian is shown by what Paul, the writer of Galatians, calls the fruit of the Spirit. The fruit of the Spirit are 'love, joy, peace, patience, kindness, goodness, faithfulness, gentleness and self-control' (Galatians 5: 22–23). What Paul means by this is that just as an apple tree produces apples, so Christians who have the Holy Spirit in them should show this by the attitudes they have. The Bible also records the gifts of the Spirit. These are the talents that God may give his followers through the presence of the Holy Spirit in their lives, and they include the gift of healing, miraculous powers and teaching.

Baptism with the Holy Spirit

In Matthew 3: 11, John the Baptist tells people that he baptises with water but that Jesus will baptise with the Holy Spirit and fire. Christians today have different views about what the Bible means when it talks of being baptised in the Spirit. Some Christians believe that when people accept Jesus as their saviour and they repent of their sins, they become part of the Church, also known as the Body of Christ. They believe that the Holy Spirit lives in them and works through them in the ways described in the Bible. Other Christians believe that when the baptism of the Holy Spirit happens people have become Christian and it empowers them to serve God, just like the apostles waited 50 days until Pentecost before the Holy Spirit empowered them to speak in Jerusalem. For these Christians the baptism of the Holy Spirit may lead them to speak and pray in heavenly languages unknown to themselves and others; the Bible calls this the gift of tongues.

Link it up

1 Read the Bible bitz and list the different roles and words used when describing the Holy Spirit.

2 For those who believe they have received the gift of the Holy Sprit what visible difference would you expect it to make in their lives? Use the list you have just created and the information on these pages to help you answer this question.

3 Using your work from 1 and 2 describe how God has intervened in the world through the Holy Spirit.

Bible bitz

When he comes, he will convict the world of guilt in regard to sin and righteousness and judgement: in regard to sin, because men do not believe in me; in regard to righteousness, because I am going to the Father, where you can see me no longer; and in regard to judgement, because the prince of this world now stands condemned.

I have much more to say to you, more than you can now bear. But when he, the Spirit of truth, comes, he will guide you into all truth.

John 16: 8–13

We are witnesses of these things, and so is the Holy Spirit, whom God has given to those who obey him.

Acts 5: 32

… God has poured out his love into our hearts by the Holy Spirit, whom he has given us.

Romans 5: 5

You became imitators of us and of the Lord; in spite of severe suffering, you welcomed the message with the joy given by the Holy Spirit.

I Thessalonians 1: 6

For the Holy Spirit will teach you at that time what you should say.

Luke 12: 12

LET'S **RE**VISE

Christian beliefs about the nature of God

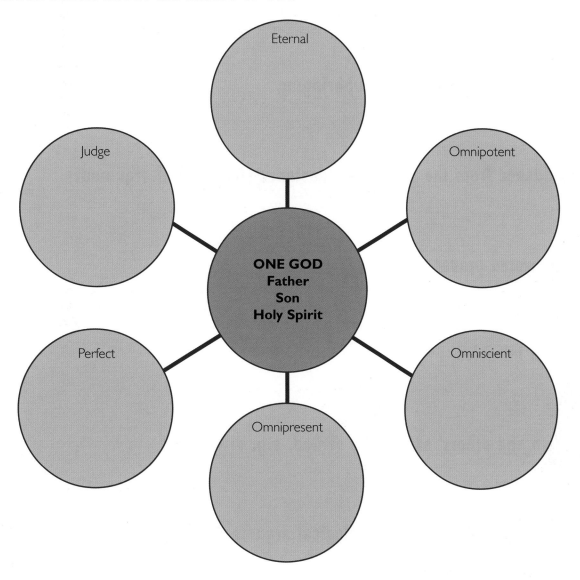

TASKS

1 Copy out the diagram. In each circle draw a symbol to represent the idea it contains. For example, you could draw a halo to represent perfection in the 'Perfect' circle, and a small circle (because a circle has no beginning or end) in the 'Eternal' circle.

2 Cover the words so you can only see the symbols. How many of the words can you now recall?

3 Try to draw the diagram from memory.

LET'S **RE**VISE

Reasons Christians give in support of their belief in God

Relatives' influence, e.g. upbringing

Evidence from the world for a designer (teleological argument)

Answered prayer

Seen miracles

Own and others' experience of God, e.g. visions

Need for a designer (cosmological argument)

TASKS

1 Use each line in the acrostic above as a heading and write a paragraph about each one.

2 Create an acrostic to help you to revise the role of the Holy Spirit.

3 Create your own revision diagram for the topic The Nature of God, for example, on:

■ the three persons of the Trinity – God the Father, Jesus the Son and the Holy Spirit

■ God intervening in the world through miracles, the person of Christ and the Holy Spirit.

LET'S **RE**VISE

Exam focus

a) What is a miracle?   *1 mark*

■ Your answer should be a short statement as to what is meant by the word 'miracle'. So you could state that it is an unexplained event which Christians believe to be an act of God.

b) What is the Holy Spirit?   *2 marks*

■ Your answer could show an idea about what the Holy Spirit is and how the Holy Spirit works. So you could say that the Holy Spirit is one of God's roles within the Trinity and that the Holy Spirit came down at Pentecost to give the disciples courage and power to teach about Jesus to the crowds in Jerusalem.

c) Describe what Christians believe about Jesus.   *3 marks*

■ Note that this question is asking a 'what' question and not a 'why' question. So you need to give different ideas about who Jesus is and what he did while on earth.

■ You could begin your answer by stating that Jesus is seen as the 'son of God' or part of the Holy Trinity and then give the reason for the 'incarnation' (why God came down in human form). You could support this idea by referring to the Bible quote John 3: 16.

■ You could give details of what Jesus did and taught while on earth or what happened to Jesus after the crucifixion.

d) Explain why Christians believe in Jesus.   *6 marks*

■ Note that this question is asking 'why' and so you will need to give different ideas on why Christians believe in Jesus. The question is *not* asking about God so do not get confused and talk about the theological proofs. The question is an 'explain' one so you should try to use the word 'because'.

■ You could start by referring to the fact that the Bible is the word of God and within the Bible there are many stories about Jesus and give an example.

■ You could refer to the fact that some Christians pray to Jesus and their prayers are answered.

■ You could refer to the idea that the disciples were willing to be martyred for their belief in Jesus and that they witnessed his resurrection.

■ You could refer to the idea that for many Christians it is not a matter of proof but faith.

e) 'If miracles were true they would happen all the time.'
Discuss this statement. You should include different, supported points of view and a
personal viewpoint. You must refer to Christianity in your answer.   *12 marks*

■ Remember – it is important to show different points of view and also your own personal point of view.

■ This question is asking you to discuss and evaluate (look at the arguments for and against) and then come to a conclusion on whether the statement is true or false. You may not want to agree or disagree entirely – that is fine but you must support your conclusion with a valid reason.

■ You may wish to show that the definition of a miracle means that it would not be a miracle if it happened all the time. Although you could refer to the fact that people have different ideas on what a miracle is and that for some people even the smallest thing, like the birth of a new baby, is a miracle.

■ You could refer to the different Christian ideas and beliefs on miracles and link them to relevant events in the Bible or modern-day examples.

■ Remember to include your own personal viewpoint.

TOPIC 2 Religious and Spiritual Experience

Key Concepts

In this topic you will learn about:

- Worship in the church and at home
- The use and significance of symbolism in worship
- The use of art and music to express beliefs about God
- PRAYER and meditation
- Food and FASTING.

Christians believe that they can develop spiritually through worship, becoming closer to God. Worship means to give worth to God. Christians may worship together, during church services every Sunday, for example, and also in quiet times alone through prayer and meditation.

Christians have many aids that they may use in worship, including praying in order to communicate with God and to deepen their relationship with him. They believe that prayer is powerful because God chooses to act in response to it. A central element of most Christian worship is the act of communion, the sharing of bread and wine, but at other times Christians might fast to help bring them closer to God.

Worship in the church and at home

TASKS

Complete the first three tasks on your own and in silence.

1 List all the good things about your school.

2 List the ways in which you contribute to the life of your school. This can include how you treat your school environment and your attitude to others as well as the activities that you take part in.

3 Consider what you could do that would make a positive difference to either your school environment or the life of the school.

4 Either in pairs or small groups, discuss your answers to the first three questions. Produce a set of answers in your group and feed them back to the whole class.

5 Now as a class decide on the top three ideas that would make a positive difference to your school environment.

6 As a class, list:
- the benefits of completing the tasks on your own
- the benefits gained from going over the task in small groups
- the benefits of coming together as a whole class to make decisions.

Worship is a word from middle English which means to give worthiness, honour and worth. The Christian concept of worship is the recognising of God's worth primarily through various forms of prayer, music and PREACHING which is applied to daily living. Through Christian worship, God is given the PRAISE and ADORATION that Christians believe he is worthy of. For Christians worship is an act of love in response to God.

Christians do not worship only as part of a large CONGREGATION at church on a Sunday; they also worship alone and they might meet for worship in small groups. Each type of worship helps Christians in a different way, just as there were different benefits to be gained from completing the above tasks in various ways.

COMMUNAL worship

Christians usually go to worship at church on a Sunday with other people. Sunday services take on different formats at different churches. Some churches are more formal in style than others and use set patterns for their services. This is known as LITURGICAL worship. In this form of service the congregation responds to the minister by reading set words from a service sheet or book. Both the Catholic Church and the Church of England use liturgical worship.

Other church services are non-liturgical, which means they may be more spontaneous and have little pre-organised structure. In such services anyone in the congregation might be invited to pray, choose a hymn or SPEAK IN TONGUES.

Most Christian services have some common features such as hymns, prayers, Bible readings and a SERMON. Church services can also include HOLY COMMUNION, which may take place weekly, fortnightly or less regularly.

Hymns

Hymns are words of worship set to music, and the style of music varies greatly. There may be a traditional accompaniment provided by an organ, or a more modern accompaniment from a church band that includes drums and guitars. The words of the hymns allow worshippers to communicate with God together, which provides a sense of unity. The words may express a variety of responses to God, including love, thankfulness and remorse.

At Your Feet We Fall

At your feet we fall,
Mighty risen Lord,
As we come before your throne to worship you.
By your Spirit's power
You now draw our hearts,
And we hear your voice of triumph ringing clear.
I am he that liveth,
That liveth and was dead.
Behold,
I am alive for evermore.

Dave Fellingham (Copyright © Thank You Music)

TASKS

1 Read through the lyrics to the hymn on the left. They include poetic phrases that need to be understood in order for the hymn to have meaning. What do you think are meant by the following phrases?
   - 'At your feet we fall'
   - 'You now draw our hearts'
   - 'I am he that liveth and was dead'

2 From the list below, what category would you place this hymn in and why?
   - Praise
   - Thankfulness
   - Repentance
   - Reflection

3 Go to www.hymnlyrics.org and select the lyrics of another hymn. Repeat the first two tasks above for the lyrics that you have selected.

Bible reading

The Bible is read aloud in church services, by readers standing at the front of the congregation, or in a dramatised way. Worshippers can think about what the reading means and often the minister will refer to it in the sermon. Many denominations, including the Church of England and the Catholic Church, follow a pattern for Bible readings throughout the year.

Sermons

During a service the minister or speaker will give a talk, which is called the sermon. The person PREACHING may link what they are saying to particular Bible passages, a current issue or a specific area of Christian DOCTRINE such as forgiveness. Through the sermon, Christians hope to understand what God is saying to them and how it may apply to their lives. The sermon might give an individual encouragement in a time of difficulty, guidance on a decision that needs to be made, or a challenge to apply something that they have heard to their lives.

TASKS

4 Explain whether you think it is helpful for a church to follow a set pattern of Bible readings each year.

5 How do you think listening to a sermon might benefit a Christian?

Holy Communion

At the service of Holy Communion, bread and the wine are shared out just as Jesus commanded his disciples to do at the Last Supper (Matthew 26: 26–29). The broken bread represents the body of Christ and the wine represents his blood that was shed on the cross.

In the Catholic Church and the Church of England Holy Communion is a SACRAMENT – a special action through which God is present with his people. Catholics believe in TRANSUBSTANTIATION. This is the belief that a change takes place in the bread and the wine and they become the body and blood of Jesus, even though they appear outwardly unchanged. ANGLICANS believe in what is known as the real presence, meaning that Christ is specially present in the bread and the wine – they are more than SYMBOLS, but the Church of England does not explain it any further. For other Christians Holy Communion is completely symbolic. It is a reminder of what Christ did by dying on the cross and of his continued presence with them now.

Prayers

Prayers are an important part of worship in the church. See pages 43–45 for more on prayers in worship.

See pages 43–45 for more on prayers in worship.

TASK

6 Explain the different ways in which Christians might understand Holy Communion. In your answer use the phrases 'transubstantiation' and the 'real presence'.

EXAM FOCUS ...

Explain how Christians might worship God together in a place of worship.

question d), 6 marks

... HINTS

- This question is asking you to show how and why Christians worship God together. So make sure you address both the how and the why.
- Note the question is not specifically talking about a church so you could talk about a chapel or meeting house (Quakers) or citadel (Salvation Army) if you wished.
- There are many different ways in which Christians worship God and you may wish to refer to several examples or explain one in depth.
- Remember to show the reasons why Christians worship together rather than on their own. You could refer to the idea that they are following the example of the early Christians or that they feel by worshipping together their faith is strengthened by the community spirit.

Jesus took the bread, gave thanks and broke it, and gave it to his disciples, saying, 'Take and eat; this is my body.' Then he took the cup, gave thanks, and offered it to them, saying, 'Drink from it, all of you. This is my blood of the COVENANT, which is poured out for many for the forgiveness of SINS.'

Matthew 26: 26–29

The Last Supper by Leonardo da Vinci

STRETCH WHAT YOU KNOW

The painting of the Last Supper by Leonardo da Vinci specifically focuses on the reaction of the disciples when Jesus says that one of them is going to betray him. It is based on the biblical account of John 13: 21.

1 Explain in your own words the different reactions of each of the disciples in the painting to Jesus' claim that one of them will betray him.

2 What is it about the painting that ALLUDES to the TRINITY?

3 Sketch your own picture of the Last Supper based on Matthew 26, the painting by Leonardo da Vinci and any other artists' versions of the Last Supper that you can research on the internet.

4 Explain why you have presented your sketch in the way that you have.

Private worship

Often Christians will spend some time each day in their own private worship. This quiet time might include prayer and Bible reading with the help of a study book. Bible study books usually have a suggested reading for the day and then an explanation of the meaning of that particular passage of the Bible. They might also contain questions relating to the Bible reading for people to think through on their own or within a group. Using another book alongside the Bible can help Christians to understand the Bible or their FAITH better.

The use and significance of symbolism in worship

Here are three well-known images:

British Red Cross

To discuss

1   What do you understand from each symbol shown above?

2   How would you redesign one of the symbols above to make it more effective in conveying the meaning of what it represents?

3   Why do people use symbols instead of words? Which do you think is more effective?

SYMBOLS instantly convey a message or meaning to those who are familiar with them. A simple image can sometimes express what would otherwise take many words to say. For example, the British Red Cross logo is the symbol of a charitable non-religious organisation responding to conflicts and natural disasters in the UK and overseas. The red cross emblem on its own is used by military medical services and others as a sign of neutrality and protection during armed conflicts. Christianity also makes use of symbols to represent aspects of the Christian faith. Christian symbols are seen in different places within a church, such as on the altar, on candles, carved into brickwork, and on stained glass. Christians sometimes display symbols on their cars or in their homes, too, as an expression and reminder of their belief. The most well-known and important Christian symbol is the cross or CRUCIFIX.

Symbolism also forms a regular and important part of Christian worship.

Symbolism in worship

During infant baptism there is a significant amount of symbolism used in order to reinforce the meaning of what is happening. In the Catholic Church and the Church of England infant baptism involves water from the font poured over the child's head, the priest says the baby's name and baptises him or her in the name of the Father, Son and Holy Spirit. The use of water symbolises being cleansed of ORIGINAL SIN and the beginning of new life. Catholics rub blessed oil, called chrism, on the child's forehead to symbolise the coming of the Holy Spirit to begin quietly working in the child's life. The priest may light a candle from the PASCHAL CANDLE and hand it to the parents to represent moving from spiritual darkness to light.

In some non-conformist Churches, for example Baptist Churches, it is adults that are baptised rather than children. The act of adult or believers' baptism is symbolic of an individual's freewill choice to become a Christian. The adult will have repented of his or her sin and committed to follow the Christian faith. The believer stands about waist deep in a pool of water in a church (a BAPTISMAL POOL), although sometimes it may even be the sea or a river. The believer will often wear white to symbolise the forgiveness from sin received from God because of faith in Christ. The adult is asked by the minister leading the service to proclaim repentence of sin and commitment to the Christian faith. The minister then lays the believer fully back under the water saying 'I baptise you in the name of the Father, the Son and the Holy Spirit' before lifting the person back up to standing. By being taken under the water the believer is symbolising the death to sin and the disobedience towards God. As the believer is raised back up it is representing being brought into a new life with faith in God and the presence of the Holy Spirit. As with infant baptism, the water itself symbolises the cleansing work of God.

Holy communion is a regular part of worship in Catholic and Anglican Churches and is full of symbolism and is very important to believers. During communion Christians take and eat a small piece of bread and a small glass of wine. Jesus commanded his disciples to do this during the Last Supper. In the Church of England this is called the eucharist, from a Greek word meaning 'thanksgiving'. The bread represents the body of Jesus and the wine represents his blood. During eucharist Jesus is believed to be spiritually present in the bread and the wine, as his SACRIFICE is celebrated. In the Catholic Church the bread is called the host, from the Latin for victim, as it represents Jesus. Unlike the Church of England, Catholics believe in TRANSUBSTANTIATION. This means that they believe that a change occurs in the bread and wine that makes them the body and blood of Jesus although their appearance remains the same.

In Catholic Churches and some Anglican Churches there is a container of holy water, blessed by the priest, near the entrance of the church. As people come in to worship they dip their fingers in the water and make the sign of the cross. By doing this they are affirming their baptism. Water is also a reminder of God's purity and his life-giving power.

During worship these churches may also burn incense. The incense is put in a container called a censer and wafted round during a service. It creates a sweet-smelling aroma that is meant to symbolise the prayers from worshippers going up to God.

Symbolism used in worship in this way engages many of the worshippers' senses and can add meaning to their experience of worship.

TASK

1 Take a piece of paper:

- Divide your page into three columns as shown below
- Work through the examples on this page and sort the information into the three columns
- The first example has been done for you:

Worship	Symbolism	Significance
use of incense	sweet smells wafting upwards	reminder of prayers going up to God

2 How may using a range of senses in worship add meaning to the worshipper's experience?

1 Do you associate colours with feelings? What examples can you give?

2 How effective do you think the symbolic use of colours is for helping worshippers to relate to specific times in the Christian calendar?

3 In what way do you think the use of colours may help to remind Christians of the significance of certain times in the year?

Liturgical colours

The symbolic use of colour is important in both the Church of England and the Catholic Church. They both use different colours throughout the LITURGICAL YEAR to represent different events and reflect the spirit of a particular season. The different colours are shown in the priest's clothes (vestments) and in the altar cloths. Some examples from the Catholic Church are given below.

The symbolic use of colour is important in both the Church of England and the Catholic Church and it is tied in with the Church year and the use of liturgy to understand the ministry and mystery of Christ fully human and yet fully God. Liturgies celebrated during the different seasons of the liturgical year have distinctive music and specific readings, prayers and rituals. All of these work together to reflect the spirit of the particular season. The colours of the vestments that the priest wears during the liturgy also help express the character of the mysteries being celebrated.

	White is seen to represent purity and completeness and is also recognised as the colour of joy and victory. It is used for the seasons of Christmas and Easter, both times of celebration in the Church as God's incarnation and then his RESURRECTION are remembered.
	Red (the colour of blood) is used on days when Christians celebrate the passion of Jesus on Passion Sunday and Good Friday. Red (the colour of fire) recalls the Holy Spirit and is used on PENTECOST and for the SACRAMENT of Confirmation.
	Green, seen everywhere in plants and trees, symbolises life and hope and is used during Ordinary Time. Ordinary Time is the two periods of time in the Christian calendar: the first is the time after Epiphany until Ash Wednesday and the second is after Pentecost up until Advent.
	During the time of Jesus purple dye was very expensive, was only affordable for the wealthy and often worn by royalty. The colour purple is used at Advent to help Christians to remember that they are preparing for the coming of Jesus, God on earth who is the ultimate Lord. Purple is also used during Lent.
	Rose may be used on the Third Sunday of Advent, and on the Fourth Sunday of Lent. It expresses the joy of anticipation for Christmas and Easter,

EXAM FOCUS ...

Explain how Christians might use symbols to express belief

question d), 6 marks

... HINTS

■ This question is asking you to explain how a symbol is used and what that symbol represents. It is in fact a question of two parts so make sure you address this. So, for instance, you might like to refer to the cross which is the main symbol of Christianity. You would state how the cross is used, for example, worn around the neck, and why it is used, to show the death and resurrection of Jesus.

■ You could refer to the many symbols shown above or you might like to refer to the way food is used as a symbol in Christian worship and festivals.

1 Draw each of the Christian symbols shown below down the left-hand side of your page.
2 Identify and then copy or summarise the correct explanation, a)–e), next to each symbol.

Symbols in church buildings

Churches often have symbols in them which help believers to reflect on their beliefs or their understanding of God in their own personal worship of him.

a) This symbol is often seen on KNEELERS in churches, in stained glass or around church buildings. It can be used to symbolise different things. Often, it is used to represent God's Spirit as he appeared during the baptism of Jesus, a reminder of his presence with his people. To some Christians it is a symbol of peace.

c) The chi-rho is made up of two Greek letters that are at the start of the word for Christ: Χριστος

Combined, they often look similar to a cross.

b) ΙΧΘΥΣ is Greek for 'fish'. Each letter of this word is the first letter in Greek of the words 'Jesus Christ, Son of God, Saviour'. The early Christians used to draw the symbol of a fish to identify themselves to one another; those who were not Christians did not understand what the symbol meant. In this way Christians hoped to avoid identification and arrest by those who were aiming to persecute them.

d) These are the first and last letters of the Greek alphabet, alpha and omega. This symbol is often on candles in churches, such as those lit during baptismal services. It is a reminder to Christians that God is the beginning and end of all things.

e) A cross with an image of Jesus upon it is called a crucifix. The crucifix focuses thoughts on Jesus' sacrifice through his death on the cross. This sacrifice and forgiveness of sins is celebrated through Holy Communion. A simple cross not only helps believers to recall Christ's death but also his resurrection, through which death was overcome. This symbol is the most important for Christians as its meaning is central to all other Christian belief.

The use of music and art to express beliefs about God

Music

To discuss

1 What is happening in each of the photos above? What do you think the atmosphere is like at each place?

2 What is the obvious difference between the singing done in each of these places?

3 Why do fans act in this way at a rugby match?

4 What similarities are there between the fans' behaviour at the rugby match and the behaviour of the worshippers in the church?

Music in COMMUNAL worship helps bring the worshippers together and provides a way of allowing the CONGREGATION to express themselves to God as one body. This experience has been compared to the 'worship' fans offer their team at a football match, when they join together in singing and chanting familiar songs.

Christian music is as diverse as any other form of music. It includes traditional hymns accompanied by an organ, modern songs supported by a band, and gospel choirs, as well as rock, pop and rap music. Sometimes the music used in worship is completely instrumental and is used to aid meditation. At other times the words are a way for believers to express their thoughts and feelings about God to him as an act of worship. A worshipper should agree with the words they are singing, as they are being sung directly to God.

Lorraine

Music is a really important part of my worship to God. I find that it is not only the words of hymns and songs that help me to express my beliefs about him but also the music itself. My favourite traditional hymn is called 'How Great Thou Art' and it is a very powerful and triumphant piece of music; this to me reflects the power and greatness of God. The words in the hymn compliment this when they speak of how by just looking at the world God has created we can see his glory. In contrast to this I also find the song 'Abba, Father' a very expressive way of communicating my relationship with God. Once again the style of music says as much as the words. The music is slow and calm allowing the worshipper to call out to God. The words themselves speak of the intimate relationship I believe I have with God, so close that I can call him 'abba', meaning daddy.

I also love considering God through art, both art by others that I can look at and unravel, but also art that I create as an expression of my own beliefs about God. The great thing about art is that each of us can understand it and access it in our own way. I find it helpful to think about God through art from around the world. For example, in African art Jesus has been portrayed as a tribal chief, showing his authority over his people. Other art that I find particularly expressive of the nature of God is abstract art by people such as Cornelis Monsma and Paul Myhill. The colours and shapes create a sense of the heart and character of God that I struggle to put into words.

TASKS

1. What music do you listen to and how does it help you to express yourself?
2. Lorraine talks about how the various styles of Christian music help to express beliefs about God. Using the information about music explain how music can help to express the nature of God.
3. Go to www.ucb.co.uk and find out what programmes this Christian radio station offers and who it is aimed at. Why do you think UCB offer a range of programmes containing different styles of Christian music?
4. Lorraine explains that art from countries around the world often shows Jesus as a man from their own culture. Why do you think this is?
5. In what way may art help a person express their faith in a way that words cannot?

Art

Art can be seen in many churches and some people find it helpful in worship as a way of expressing Christian beliefs about God. Art may take many forms, such as sculpture, needlework, stained glass and carvings. The varied responses that the art might inspire could lead a person into a deeper sense of knowledge of God. The use of art varies between denominations. For example, ORTHODOX churches are highly decorated, Catholic and ANGLICAN churches often have stained glass windows and KNEELERS and sculptures while non-conformist churches may be devoid of any form of art.

Icons

Orthodox churches are highly decorated with icons, which often include rich colours and gold. This use of expensive but natural materials is in itself a means of expressing an aspect of their belief about God. God is believed to be worthy of these costly artist creations; he is worth more than even the gold used in the icons. Icons are produced using all natural materials taken from the world created by God. The art itself therefore speaks of the creator God who meets all human needs.

Stained-glass windows

Stained-glass windows often depict stories from the Bible. These pieces of art may reinforce the beliefs about God in a literal way, showing his power through MIRACLES or his sacrificial love when dying on the cross. The use of light is often very powerful in stained glass as a means of representing beliefs about God. For example, the blue window at Buckfast Abbey with the image of Jesus at the last supper includes a halo which shines boldly as the light hits it, reminding believers of his divinity even when he came to earth in the form of Jesus. Light is a powerful metaphor for the nature of God as it may be alluding to any number of beliefs about him including his purity, his knowledge and his righteousness. One artist who famously uses light in his work to show the presence of God in the world is Thomas Kincaid.

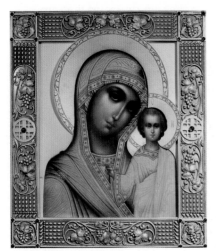

The Virgin Kazanskaya by Dmitrii Smirnov. A Russian Orthodox icon, c.1915.

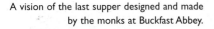

A vision of the last supper designed and made by the monks at Buckfast Abbey.

Absence of art

The absence of art in some churches is itself an expression of belief about God. Some Churches and Christians believe that because God is beyond anything we have experienced, any image of him will be insufficient and a distraction to any worship of him. God alone is to be worshipped and some Christians believe that if art was in their churches it may be possible that artistic images would become the focus of worship rather than the one true God.

1 Working on your own, briefly describe each of the pieces of art (A–D).
2 Explain how each piece could help a Christian in their spiritual life and in their worship.
3 Which piece of art do you:
- most like?
- most dislike?
Explain why.

Art as an expression of worship by the artist

Art is also an expression of worship by the artists themselves. An artist might:

- stitch a kneeler that others will use for PRAYER
- design a stained-glass window that depicts aspects of life in the church community, or beliefs and stories from the Bible. These images enable people of all ages and abilities to respond to them.

A Station of the Cross painted on ceramic tiles outside St John the Baptist church, Majorca.

Rows of church kneelers.

Yellow Christ by Paul Gauguin (1848–1903), 1889.

To discuss

5 Compare your answers to the above tasks with another person or small group in your class. How do they differ?

6 Why do you think people differ in both their understanding of art and their preferences?

7 In what ways might the fact that art is open to personal interpretation be helpful in Christian worship?

Crucifixion by the contemporary US artist Spencer Williams.

STRETCH WHAT YOU KNOW

A good example of Christian sculpture can be seen at Wintershall, a privately owned area of land in Surrey. At Wintershall visitors can walk past the STATIONS OF THE CROSS, with each station a sculpture created by a different artist. For some Christians the combination of being surrounded by the created world and the stations in such a range of styles adds to their understanding of who God is. It helps people to reflect deeply and can offer them a new perspective on the final hours of the life of Christ.

1 Go to www.bbc.co.uk/religion/galleries/stations/ and find out what is shown at each of the Stations of the Cross.

2 Select one of the stations and design your own sculpture for it.

3 Explain what your design is saying about the character or work of God through Jesus.

One of the Stations of the Cross sculptures at Wintershall in Surrey. The Wintershall Estate holds a Life of Christ play during the last week of June, which attracts 6000 people a day including large numbers of stiudents and their teachers.

EXAM FOCUS ...

'Music and religious pictures help people to worship God.'

Discuss this statement. You should include different, supported points of view and a personal viewpoint. You must refer to Christianity in your answer.

question e), 12 marks

... HINTS

■ Remember – it is important to show different points of view and also your own personal point of view.

■ This question is asking you to discuss and evaluate (look at the arguments for and against) and then come to a conclusion on whether the statement is true or false. You may not want to agree or disagree entirely – that is fine but you must support your conclusion with a valid reason. Remember to give examples of both music and art in your answer.

■ You could refer to the fact that some Christians like plain places of worship with no statues and pictures as they think it distracts from worshipping God.

■ You could refer to places of worship that contain many images and pictures because these are an aid to help people focus or are used to glorify God.

■ You could refer to the different types of music used in Christian worship and contrast these with Mother Teresa's or the Quakers' ideas of silence in order to listen to God.

■ Remember to add your own personal view.

Prayer and meditation

The purpose and use of prayer to deepen faith

Prayer is another way in which Christians believe they can communicate with God. Just as it is important to talk to people in order to develop your relationship with them, Christians believe that prayer helps them to develop their relationship with God.

Sometimes, prayers in church services are led by one person – or by several people – and the CONGREGATION are invited to take part through set responses, such as 'Lord, hear our prayer'. At other times, the congregation may simply listen to the prayers and then confirm their agreement with all that has been said by saying 'AMEN' at the end. In some church services any member of the congregation who wishes to stand and pray aloud is free to do so. Services can also include times for silent prayer, which allow people a period of reflection.

In the Bible Jesus taught his followers how to pray by giving them what is now known as the Lord's Prayer. The prayer includes CONFESSION, thankfulness for all God gives us, ADORATION of him, concern for others, and SUPPLICATION. In church services the words of the Lord's Prayer are often said aloud by everyone.

The Lord's Prayer

Our Father in heaven,
HALLOWED be your name,
your kingdom come,
your will be done
on earth as it is in heaven.
Give us today our daily bread.
Forgive us our sins,
As we forgive those who sin against us
And lead us not into temptation,
But deliver us from the evil one.

Matthew 6: 9–13

TASKS

One way to remember the pattern of prayer that is used by Christians and is seen in the Lord's Prayer is to use the acrostic STOP. Just think 'Christians STOP to pray'.

S orry
T hanks (and adoration)
O thers
P lease

1 Copy out the STOP acrostic above. Use each of the four words as headings and under each one either:
   - write the parts from the Lord's Prayer that fit that heading, or
   - create your own example of a prayer that follows the STOP pattern.

2 Divide a piece of paper into two columns as shown below:

Benefits of set prayer	Problems with set prayer

Place each of the ideas below in the column you think it belongs in:
   - Gives a sense of unity to the congregation.
   - Does not allow individuals to express themselves in their own way.
   - May not relate to current issues in the life of the church or individuals.
   - Gives people the words to say if they find praying aloud difficult.
   - The prayer may become more familiar if used regularly, for example the Lord's Prayer.

   Add other ideas to each column if you can.

3 Using the ideas from task 2, explain whether you think it is helpful for Christians to have set words to say for prayer.

Bible bitz

You who call on the Lord, give yourselves no rest, and give him no rest till he establishes Jerusalem and makes her the praise of the earth.

Isaiah 62: 6–7

Do not be anxious about anything, but in everything, by prayer and petition, with thanksgiving, present your requests to God.

Philippians 4: 5–7

Be joyful always; pray continually; give thanks in all circumstances, for this is God's will for you in Christ Jesus.

I Thessalonians 5

The prayer offered in faith will make the sick person well; the Lord will raise him up. If he has sinned, he will be forgiven. Therefore confess your sins to each other and pray for each other so that you may be healed. The prayer of a righteous man is powerful and effective.

James 5: 15–16

The eyes of the Lord are on the righteous and his ears are attentive to their prayer.

I Peter 3: 12

Link it up

1 What reasons do the Bible quotes give for Christians to pray?
2 According to the Bible who is it that hears and answers prayers?
3 What reasons may Christians give to explain the power of prayer based on these verses?

EXAM FOCUS ...

Explain how praying every day might help Christians in their daily lives.

question d), 6 marks

Prayer and meditation

When Christians pray alone in private worship they will usually use the four different areas of prayer (Sorry, Thanks, Others, Please – see page 43), but they give priority to the issues they most want to speak to God about.

Often, Christians will pray regularly for people whom they know, or for work in which they have a particular interest, such as the work of a charity. Christians may also be aware of how God is working in their own lives day by day and so they can respond to him with personal thanks and PRAISE. They might seek God's help, guidance or encouragement for particular challenges in their own lives, too – issues that are not relevant to everyone involved in public worship at a church service. For example, a person considering a change of career might seek God's help in guiding them to the right decision. By regularly praying to God and meditating on his word Christians' reliance on him increases and their FAITH is deepened as they seek his will in all aspects of their lives.

Christians will often spend time alone in silent reflection or meditation, being still and calm and considering what they believe God is saying to them. Meditation gives Christians the opportunity to feel at peace.

Private worship is important to many Christians because it helps them to develop a close and personal relationship with God.

The power of prayer and answered prayer

As Christians pray to God they believe he hears and responds to their prayers. In the Bible God commands his people to pray in a way that reflects his teachings and he promises to hear and answer such prayers. There are powerful examples in the Bible that illustrate the Christian belief that prayer changes things. For example, when the Israelites fight the Amalakites as God tells them to, Moses holds his hands up and prays to God for Israel's victory. As Moses tires and lowers his hands the Amalakites take control of the battle, Aaron and Hur help Moses to hold his hands up and the Israelites win the battle (Exodus 17).

It is with prayer that Jesus brought Lazarus back from the dead in John 11 and in calling on Jesus' name Peter and John healed a crippled beggar. Both are examples of the power that Christians believe that prayer has.

Many Christians today can give examples of how prayer has powerfully affected situations or people that they have prayed for. This belief in the power of prayer is shown in the 24–7 prayer movement which responds to Jesus' command to his followers to pray day and night in Luke 18 (see the Case Study opposite). 24–7 prayer was unplanned; it started in September 1999, when a group of young people in England decided to pray non-stop for a month. They didn't stop until Christmas! From there the prayer meeting has spread to many nations, denominations and age groups. Hundreds of non-stop prayer meetings now link up on the internet to form a chain of prayer.

... HINTS

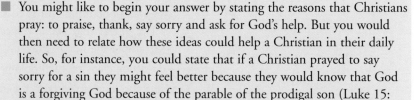

■ You might like to begin your answer by stating the reasons that Christians pray: to praise, thank, say sorry and ask for God's help. But you would then need to relate how these ideas could help a Christian in their daily life. So, for instance, you could state that if a Christian prayed to say sorry for a sin they might feel better because they would know that God is a forgiving God because of the parable of the prodigal son (Luke 15: 11–32).

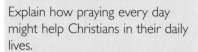

Case Study: 24–7 Prayer

What are the aims?

To turn the tide. The dream behind 24–7 is to turn the tide of youth culture back to Jesus. Something has to change. That is why God is mobilising prayer movements like 24–7 (and others).

We're seeing thousands of young people from Alaska to Australia praying together for their friends and their heroes in a focused and persistent way. 24–7 targets youth culture at a local, national and international level; addressing demographies (like skaters and clubbers) as well as geographies (schools, communities, nations).

> *'Pray continually.' (Jesus)*
> *'WOW! This prayer thing actually WORKS!'*
> *(Shocked student)*

Why?

Because bold, persistent prayer is effective. First it changes us. Then it changes the world.

- Pentecost came to a prayer room.
- Paul urged the Thessalonians to 'pray constantly'.
- The early Church 'joined together constantly in prayer' (Acts 1–14).
- Celtic Monks at Bangor Abbey in Ireland prayed continually for 200 years. A young Celt called Ciaran formed a community in Clonmacnoise near Dublin back in 547CE. Sadly Ciaran died after just seven months but the community prayed for about 1000 years and sent out missionaries all over the world!
- The Pope decreed continual prayer in certain locations in the fifteenth century.
- In the eighteenth century, a small community of Moravians began a 24–7 prayer meeting that lasted for over 100 years, mobilised 3000 missionaries and converted John Wesley!

(From the 24–7 Prayer website: www.24-7prayer.com)

TASKS

1 What culture is 24–7 aimed at and who does it say it is reaching?
2 Why do 24–7 aim to pray in a persistent and focused way?
3 Give two examples from history that show the Christian commitment to prayer.
4 24–7 says that prayer first changes the individual and then the world. How do you think Christians believe prayer changes them and how may this affect the world?

Why pray?

Because we need miracles more than we need strategies
Because the world is a vacuum waiting to be filled
Because the MTV generation is lost in space
Because we've seen the end of the movie
Because this is not the dress rehearsal
Because the poor are getting poorer
Because we're aliens in the world
Because we're too sensible
Because boredom is sin
Because he's
worth it

www.24-7prayer.com

To discuss

1 What do you think is meant by each line in the quote above about prayer?
2 To what extent do you agree that pray has the power to make a difference in all these areas?
3 If prayer is not communication with God what else could it be? Can this also explain the changes that are said to occur as a result of prayer?

Jesus sent Peter and John, saying, 'Go and make preparations for us to eat the Passover.'

Luke 22: 8

The Lord Jesus, on the night he was betrayed, took bread, and when he had given thanks, he broke it and said, 'This is my body, which is for you; do this in remembrance of me.' In the same way, after supper he took the cup, saying, 'This cup is the new covenant in my blood; do this, whenever you drink it, in remembrance of me.' For whenever you eat this bread and drink this cup, you proclaim the Lord's death until he comes.

I Corinthians 11: 23–26

To discuss

Look at the items represented below and on page 47.

1 Which group of items would you find it hardest to go without for 40 days? Why?

2 Are there other items that you would find it even more difficult to go without for 40 days? Why?

3 Is there any reason that would make you willing to give up these items? Explain your answer.

Food and fasting

Fasting

Fasting is the act of choosing to go without food, drink or both for a period of time. For Christians one purpose of fasting is to maintain complete dependence on God and to put nothing in a more important place than him in their daily lives.

Many Christians choose to fast although it is not a compulsory part of their religion. Jesus fasted when he spent 40 days and 40 nights in the wilderness. During this time his commitment to honour God was tested as he resisted the temptations of the devil. He remained faithful to God and chose to give him the priority in all his decisions. For example, the devil challenged Jesus to turn stones into bread to satisfy his hunger; Jesus refused saying 'man does not live on bread alone, but on every word that comes from the mouth of God' (Matthew 4: 4).

Christians today fast for the same reasons, to show God that he comes above all other things and to confirm their total reliance on God for all they need in life. While fasting is a personal decision in the Christian faith, Jesus did give instructions on how people should fast. In Matthew, Jesus tells his followers not to proclaim to everyone their time of fasting as if boasting about their righteousness. Jesus says that fasting is a private matter between God and the individual that God himself will reward (Matthew 6: 18).

Lent

Giving up a luxury, even for just 40 days, can be very difficult because we enjoy it and are used to having it. However, many Christians choose to give up something they enjoy for 40 days each year during Lent, as part of their worship to God. Often, the treat they give up is a favourite food, such as chocolate or cake, although it can be anything.

Lent is the 40 days leading up to Easter. Many Christians believe that choosing to go without something during this time helps them to remember that they are dependent on God. God provides for their needs and gives them strength to get through life and any difficulties that they face. It is a reminder of the suffering of Jesus.

Some Christians also believe that fasting (going without certain foods) during Lent helps them to be self-disciplined, because they are exercising control over their desires. It reminds them that God alone is to be worshipped and that nothing else should have control over them. Christians might fast at other times during the year, too, in order to develop their self-discipline and increase their dependence on God as they turn to him for their needs. For some Christians fasting also reminds them not to be greedy but to be generous and aware of the needs of others.

A

TASKS

1 Read the case study below. In addition to giving up a food for Lent, what else did the campaign *Love Life Love Lent* encourage Christians to do?

2 What was the purpose behind the *Love Life Love Lent* campaign?

3 Explain whether you think having a multimedia campaign is beneficial to the celebration of Lent.

To discuss

Read the quote from the Bishop of Birmingham on the right.

4 Do you agree with the Rt Revd David Urquhart? Give reasons for your answer.

5 What changes might a Christian make to their lifestyle during the period of Lent to 'reflect God's love more fully'? Use the information in the text and about *Love Life Love Lent* to help you respond to this.

'Doing something positive or generous can be as transforming as giving something up. It helps us to reflect on how we normally behave, and how we can make changes to our lifestyles that reflect God's love more fully.'

The Rt Revd David Urquhart, Bishop of Birmingham

Case Study: *Love Life Love Lent*

The season of Lent – a period of penitence (repentance of sins) in preparation for Easter – was given an extra twist in 2006 with a multimedia campaign backed by the Archbishops of Canterbury and York, Dr Rowan Williams and Dr John Sentamu.

Love Life Love Lent gave inspiration for simple things that people could do to spread a little generosity and happiness in their community, and particularly aimed to bring Lent alive for people who might not go to church. In a bold move, the campaign was delivered through two colourful booklets, an interactive website and a text message service.

During the period of Lent, mobile phone owners could text the word 'Lent' to begin receiving daily suggestions for actions up until Easter Monday, at a price of ten pence a day. Actions included:

■ giving up your place to someone in a traffic jam or a queue

■ having a TV-free day and doing something you have meant to do for ages instead
■ taking part in an environmental clean-up
■ watching the news and praying about what you see
■ leaving a £1 coin in the shopping trolley or where someone will find it.

The actions may seem small, but can add up to something bigger when lots of people get involved. The Archbishops of Canterbury and York said in their joint introduction:

It's all too easy to feel we are powerless to make a difference. But the truth is, with God's help we can change the world a little bit each day. Each of us can be the change we want to see in the world … Together we can build better and more generous communities. Together we can lighten the load on our planet. We show God's love when we do these things.

EXAM FOCUS ...

Explain Christian beliefs about the use of food and fasting.

question d), 6 marks

Food

Unlike some other religions, there are no food laws in Christianity. Christians believe that God has allowed humans to eat plants, animals and fish (Genesis 9: 3). In the book of Acts, Peter has a vision from God, in which he is shown that no animal is unclean, or unsuitable for eating (Acts 10: 9–16). Jesus probably ate meat, just like other Jews. For example, at Passover he would have eaten lamb (Luke 22: 8). In the Bible there are also examples of Jesus helping to catch and eat fish (John 21: 11 and 13).

Christians do not usually abstain from eating any food for religious reasons. However, believing it to be part of their role as good STEWARDS of the world God has created, some Christians may carefully select the produce that they eat. For example, they might eat meat only from animals that have been kept in good living conditions before they were slaughtered, or eat only eggs produced by free-range hens, because they are concerned to avoid cruelty to animals.

TASKS

4 Use the information in the text and the Bible quotes to explain why Christians do not have religious food laws.

5 Explain why some Christians might carefully select the produce that they eat. Give examples to support your answer.

6 Do you think people have a responsibility towards animals when choosing what they eat? Give reasons for your answer.

HOLY COMMUNION

Bread and wine have a symbolic meaning for Christians when they are used to celebrate Holy Communion. In such services the bread is used to represent the body of Jesus and the wine his blood that was shed on the cross. Christians continue to remember his death in this way as he commanded them to at the Last Supper (1 Corinthians 11: 23–26). The celebration of Holy Communion helps Christians to remember Jesus' presence with them.

... HINTS

- The question is asking you to explain two beliefs – one about food and the other about fasting. So make sure you answer both parts.
- You could refer to the fact that unlike other religions there are no strict food laws and support this with reference to Peter's dream (Acts 10: 9–23) but that Christians use food symbolically at the Mass or the Eucharist or Holy Communion.
- You could refer to the symbolism of Easter eggs.
- When addressing the fasting part of the question you might like to refer to the tradition that Christians give up something they like at Lent in order to give what is saved to charity. Or you may like to refer to fund raising activities such as 24-hour fasts. You could explain the significance of Lent.

LET'S **RE**VISE

Worship in the Church

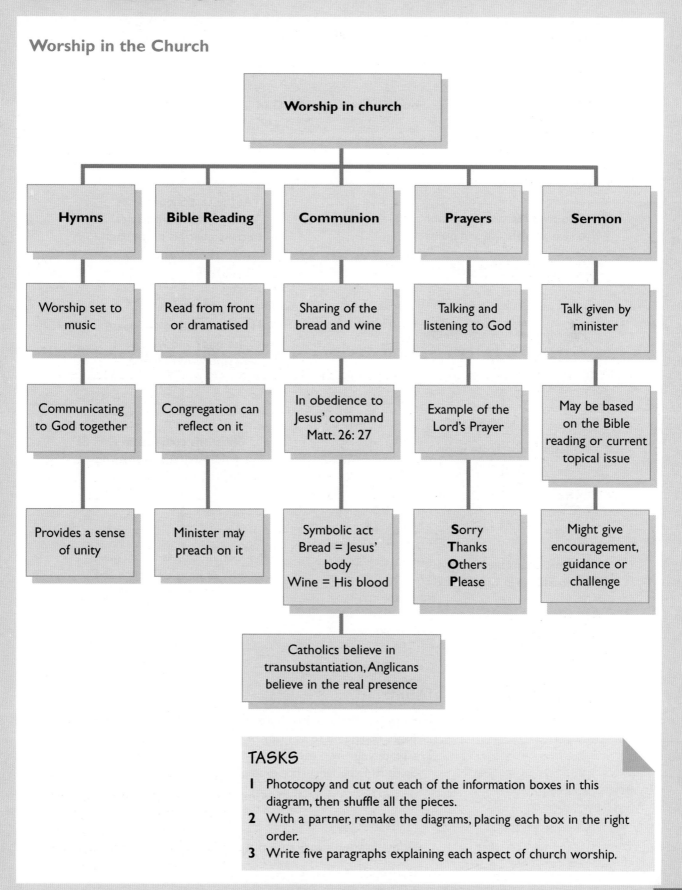

Worship in church

Hymns	Bible Reading	Communion	Prayers	Sermon
Worship set to music	Read from front or dramatised	Sharing of the bread and wine	Talking and listening to God	Talk given by minister
Communicating to God together	Congregation can reflect on it	In obedience to Jesus' command Matt. 26: 27	Example of the Lord's Prayer	May be based on the Bible reading or current topical issue
Provides a sense of unity	Minister may preach on it	Symbolic act Bread = Jesus' body Wine = His blood	**S**orry **T**hanks **O**thers **P**lease	Might give encouragement, guidance or challenge

Catholics believe in transubstantiation, Anglicans believe in the real presence

TASKS

1 Photocopy and cut out each of the information boxes in this diagram, then shuffle all the pieces.
2 With a partner, remake the diagrams, placing each box in the right order.
3 Write five paragraphs explaining each aspect of church worship.

LET'S **RE**VISE

Food as a response to God

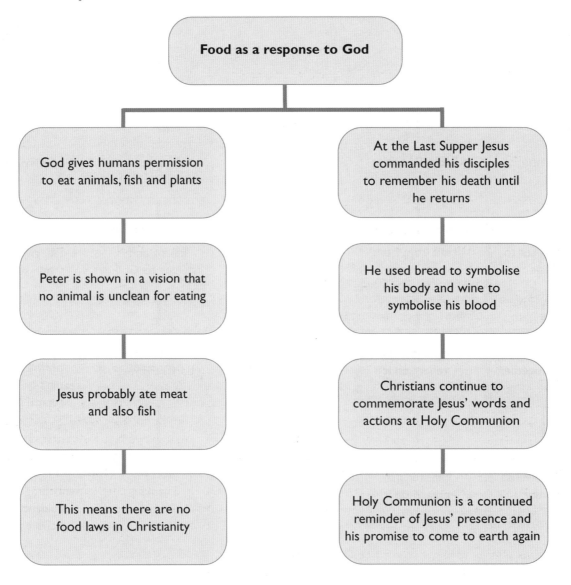

Food as a response to God

God gives humans permission to eat animals, fish and plants

Peter is shown in a vision that no animal is unclean for eating

Jesus probably ate meat and also fish

This means there are no food laws in Christianity

At the Last Supper Jesus commanded his disciples to remember his death until he returns

He used bread to symbolise his body and wine to symbolise his blood

Christians continue to commemorate Jesus' words and actions at Holy Communion

Holy Communion is a continued reminder of Jesus' presence and his promise to come to earth again

TASKS

1 Copy out the diagram above and add supporting Bible quotes from pages 46 and 48 to as many of the boxes as possible.
2 Create your own revision diagram for the topic Religious and Spiritual Experience. For example, you might include:

  ■ fasting as a response to God

  ■ the use of art and music to express beliefs about God

  ■ the use and significance of symbolism in worship.

LET'S **RE**VISE

Exam focus

a) What is fasting?   *1 mark*
- This question is asking you to give a simple definition of the word 'fasting'. So you could state it is the giving up of food for a specified amount of time.

b) Give two examples of how food is used in Christian worship.   *2 marks*
- You could give an example of food used in a festival such as Easter, or you could refer to the symbolic use of food and wine in the Eucharist.

c) Describe how music is used to express beliefs about God.   *3 marks*
- This question is asking you to give examples of different types of music which show what a Christian believes about God. So you could talk about how the Psalms in the Old Testament describe God's glory and love, for example Psalm 108. Or you could refer to Christmas carols which describe the birth of Jesus, for instance 'O little town of Bethlehem'.
- You might like to refer to more modern Christian music, but make sure you link the example to what Christians believe about God.

d) Explain how prayer is used by Christians to deepen their faith.   *6 marks*
- This question is asking you two things: what prayer is and how by praying it deepens the faith of Christians.
- You could give a short description of what prayer is: for instance 'talking' or 'communicating' with God.
- So you may like to refer to the different types of prayer and then link these up to how they strengthen faith. For instance, you could say that by saying sorry to God (penitence) this might make a Christian feel closer to God because they know he will forgive them (parable of the prodigal son).
- Or you could refer to a Christian praying to God asking him to help someone else (supplication) which when answered might strengthen their faith because God has listened to them.

e) 'For worship, prayer is more important than beautiful buildings.'
Discuss this statement. You should include different, supported points of view
and a personal viewpoint. You must refer to Christianity in your answer.   *12 marks*
- Remember – it is important to show different points of view and also your own personal point of view.
- This question is asking you to discuss and evaluate (look at the arguments for and against) and then come to a conclusion on whether the statement is true or false. You may not want to agree or disagree entirely – that is fine but you must support your conclusion with a valid reason.
- You could address this question by the fact that God is everywhere and therefore there is no need for a beautiful building to help a Christian in their prayers to God. You could support this with reference to the second commandment (no graven images).
- You might like to refer to the fact that prayer is for praising God and that a beautiful building can express this praise better than ordinary words. Try to include examples of how the architecture of a place of worship can reflect God's glory and power, such as the spire on a church.
- Remember to include your own personal view.

The End of Life

Key Concepts

In this topic you will learn about:

- Christian beliefs about the body and soul
- Christian beliefs about heaven, hell and purgatory
- Salvation, redemption and the suffering of Christ
- Relationship between God as judge, life on earth and the afterlife
- Christian funeral rites, and the ways in which these reflect belief and aim to support the bereaved.

Christians believe that humans possess a soul, also called spirit, which is distinct from the physical body. Because of this belief, they are able to believe that even though the body dies the soul can live on. Christians all agree that the soul is capable of living eternally and that God is the judge of each person after death. He will decide where each person will spend eternity. Christians believe this will be in heaven or hell. Catholics believe that some people's souls will be sent to purgatory for further PURIFICATION before they are able to enter heaven. Christian funerals reflect these beliefs and help people in the grieving process.

TASKS

1 Plato thought each of the three parts he identified played an important role in a balanced soul. Imagine three people who each relied on only one part of the soul. What do you think the effects might be for each person?

2 Think about a particular decision you have made in the last week. Can you work out how you used the three parts of the soul described by Plato in your decision-making?

Philosophical views of the soul

Case Study: *The beliefs of Plato*
The Greek PHILOSOPHER Plato (428–348BCE) thought the soul was the ESSENCE of a person, the part that makes each of us who we are as individuals. He thought it was with our soul that we decide how to act and that the soul was ETERNAL. Plato thought the soul was made up of three parts:

1 the *logos* – this is the mind, and it allows logic to be used in our decision making

2 the *thymos* – this is our emotional motive for behaving in a certain way

3 the *pathos* – this relates to our physical needs.

In a balanced soul each of these parts plays an important role.

Case Study: *The beliefs of Aristotle*
The Greek philosopher Aristotle (384–322BCE) also believed that the soul was the core essence of a being, but he argued that it didn't have a separate existence to the body. Therefore, he did not believe the soul to be eternal.

For Aristotle, human beings have bodies for rational activity, the ability to act in a reasoned way. He said that our capacity for rational activity was our essence, what makes us who we are, our soul.

This may be easier to understand using the knife example on page 53.

TASK

3 Aristotle used the ANALOGY of a knife to help explain human essence.

■ Copy the diagram on the right, filling out the human column exactly as it appears.

■ Create your own analogy to go in the left-hand column, instead of using the knife analogy.

To discuss

1 What do you think is the most important difference between Plato's view of the soul and Aristotle's? Why?

2 Which philosophical view of the soul do you agree with the most? Give reasons for your answer.

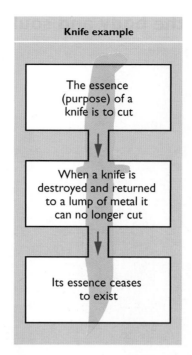

Knife example

The essence (purpose) of a knife is to cut

↓

When a knife is destroyed and returned to a lump of metal it can no longer cut

↓

Its essence ceases to exist

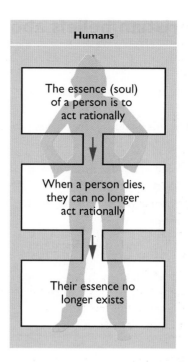

Humans

The essence (soul) of a person is to act rationally

↓

When a person dies, they can no longer act rationally

↓

Their essence no longer exists

What a person believes about the soul is likely to affect their view about death and any possible afterlife. For instance, if someone does not believe in an eternal soul then they will believe that death is the end of a person's existence.

'To the well-organised mind, death is but the next great adventure.'

Harry Potter and the Philosopher's Stone
J. K. Rowling, 1997

To discuss

3 Read the quote above from *Harry Potter*. In what way can death be seen as an adventure?

TASKS

4 List all the words or phrases Alexander Pope uses to describe the death of a person, for example, 'trembling', 'I fly'.

5 Think about the examples you have listed and then, in no more than two sentences, sum up what you think Pope's view of death was.

6 Do you think Pope's poem about death reflects J.K. Rowling's description of it as an adventure? Explain your answer.

7 Using the work you have done on Pope and Rowling to help you, write your own poem about death.

The Dying Christian to his Soul

Vital spark of heav'nly flame,
Quit, oh, quit, this mortal frame!
Trembling, hoping, ling'ring, flying,
Oh, the pain, the bliss of dying!
Cease, fond Nature, cease thy strife,
And let me languish into life!

Hark! they whisper; Angels say,
Sister Spirit, come away.
What is this absorbs me quite,
Steals my senses, shuts my sight,
Drowns my spirits, draws my breath?
Tell me, my Soul! can this be Death?

The world recedes; it disappears;
Heav'n opens on my eyes; my ears
With sounds seraphic ring:
Lend, lend your wings! I mount! I fly!
O Grave! where is thy Victory?
O Death! where is thy Sting?

Alexander Pope (1688–1744)

Christian beliefs about the body and soul

To discuss

1 Whose is the dead body being carried by Joseph of Arimathea in this picture? What makes you think this?

2 Who or what do you think is being represented by the brilliant white character in the picture?

3 What conclusions would you come to regarding Christian beliefs about the body and the soul from looking at this piece of art?

Bible bitz

The Lord God formed the man from the dust of the ground and breathed into his nostrils the breath of life, and the man became a living being.

Genesis 2: 7

So it will be with the resurrection of the dead. The body that is sown is perishable, it is raised imperishable ... it is sown a natural body, it is raised a spiritual body.

I Corinthians 15: 42 and 44

Don't you know that you yourselves are God's temple and that God's Spirit lives in you? ... for God's temple is sacred, and you are that temple.

I Corinthians 3: 16–17

When I want to do good, evil is right there with me. For in my inner being I delight in God's law ...

Romans 7: 21–22

Behold I will create new heavens and a new earth ... the wolf and the lamb will feed together ...

Isaiah 65: 17 and 25

Black Resurrection by contemporary US artist Vincent Barzoni.

Christians believe that human beings possess an IMMORTAL soul that is distinct from their physical body. Unlike the physical body, which can be observed, the soul cannot be seen. It is the possession of an immortal soul that makes human beings unique and sets us apart from all other creatures.

Christians believe that humans were made in the likeness of God (Genesis 1: 27, see page 106), who is himself ETERNAL. In Genesis 2: 7, it says that God breathed life into Adam. Thus humans received life in a different way from animals, and animals and humans are therefore distinct.

For Christians, human life is SACRED because people possess a soul. The Bible refers to the human physical body as being a temple for God in which his spirit can live (1 Corinthians 3: 16). Paul, the writer of the letter to the Corinthians, also explains that humans' imperfect and mortal bodies will die but that their spiritual bodies will be resurrected (1 Corinthians 15: 42–44). The RESURRECTION and ASCENSION of Jesus showed that there is life after a physical death.

Christians also believe that the soul and the body are often in conflict with one another. Paul writes of the body wanting to satisfy its desires and pleasures whilst the spirit wants to please God (Romans 7: 21–24).

Bible bitz

In the centre, around the throne, were four living creatures ... the first living creature was like a lion, the second like an ox, the third had a face like a man, the fourth was like a flying eagle.

Revelation 4: 6–7

Link it up

1 Using the Bible quotes above and opposite to help you, explain what Christians believe about the difference between the body and the soul.

2 Alan links the belief that only humans have souls with our ability to confess. Why do you think that having a soul may lead to confession of wrongdoings to God? Use Romans 7: 21–22 as your starting point to answer this.

TASKS

Alan says that putting humankind above the rest of creation has led to the ruined planet we have today. Answer one of the following questions:
1 Why do you think Alan has this view? Do you agree?
2 To what extent do you think the Christian concept of the soul is to blame for human beings' sense of superiority over creation?

EXAM FOCUS ...

Explain Christian beliefs about the soul.

question d), 6 marks

Alan

I have several thoughts on whether animals have souls. At the moment I have five main views.

- *The Bible is very clear that heaven is not just populated by people – see Revelation, and Isaiah 65: 25. I know these are 'pictures' but nonetheless they speak of a reality of a redeemed creation – not just mankind.*

- *All of creation is precious. Each element reflects God's glory and, therefore, has eternal significance. If a 'soul' means we have an eternal identity that goes beyond the MATERIAL, then all creation has soul.*

- *I wouldn't place too much emphasis on the Genesis references. The first comes at the end of a description of all creation – the only difference for mankind is that we are made in the image of God. We have, potentially, the same characteristics as God – this does not say anything about soul/eternal meaning. The reference in Genesis 2: 7 depicts how life comes about – all of life/creation similarly needs the 'breath of life' because without God, nothing lives.*

- *I suspect that some Christians argue that only mankind has souls because only mankind can acknowledge Jesus Christ as Lord and, therefore, receive salvation. I believe that this view is far too limiting. The life, death and resurrection of Jesus Christ have salvation implications for the whole of creation.*

- *So elevating mankind above the rest of creation is very dangerous – it has led to the plight we are facing of a ruined planet.*

... HINTS

- This question is asking you to give Christian beliefs about the soul and you should try to support these with quotes from the Bible. Since the question is asking you to explain *Christian* beliefs, if you want to discuss the Greek ideas make sure you state that these ideas have been developed by Christians otherwise you will not be credited with any marks.

- So you could begin your answer by a short definition of the soul and link it to the biblical idea of how God created Adam in Genesis 2: 7 ('the breath of life') or to the phrase 'the image of God' (Genesis 1: 27) which some Christians believe to indicate is the soul.

- You might then wish to discuss what Christians believe happens to the soul after death but do not go into too much detail because the question is not asking you about heaven and hell.

- You might wish to refer to the ideas of whether the body and soul are two separate entities or are the same.

The End of Life   **55**

Christian beliefs about heaven, hell and purgatory

TASKS

1 What impression of hell do you gain from reading the list of the nine pits?
2 Three of the nine pits are shown in the pictures below and on page 57. Create your own pictures for three more of the pits.
3 Do you think that if Dante were alive today he would add any more pits to his inferno? What would they be? Give reasons for your answer.
4 If you had lived in the fourteenth century and believed that these pits were a reality, how do you think their existence would have affected your life?
5 How useful do you think Dante's depiction of hell is in the twenty-first century? Explain your answer.

Dante's *Inferno*

In the fourteenth century the Italian poet Dante wrote a book called *Inferno*. At the start, a character named Virgil offers to give him a tour of the nine pits of hell, in each of which a different kind of sinner is punished. These are:

Pit one – Those in limbo (the unbaptised)
Pit two – The lustful
Pit three – The gluttonous
Pit four – The hoarders
Pit five – The wrathful
Pit six – The heretics
Pit seven – The violent
Pit eight – The fraudulent
Pit nine – Traitors

In the fourteenth century people believed the pits really existed and that they had been created when the angel Lucifer fell to earth and became Satan, having been thrown out of Heaven for seeking to be greater than God himself.

Pit one – those in limbo.

Pit two – the lustful.

Pit three – the gluttonous.

Christian understanding of hell

In the past Christianity did concentrate on hell as being a place of indescribable, ETERNAL torture for non-believers. The Church often used the fear of hell as a way of getting people to follow their religion. Clearly, a better understanding of our world means we know that a physical hell on earth, as depicted by Dante, does not exist. There are some Christians today who do believe that hell is a place of eternal punishment, but they also believe God to be loving and forgiving. For this reason they may try to encourage non-believers to seek out God's love, rather than trying to scare them into belief.

Other Christians have a completely different interpretation of the concept of hell. Their view is one of annihilation. Annihilation means to be completely destroyed so as to no longer exist. In this view hell is when the body and the soul both cease to exist at the point of physical death.

Many Christians believe that hell is a way of expressing an eternal existence without God's presence and blessing. These Christians see the biblical descriptions of hell as being symbolic – an aid to help people grasp a very difficult idea. Clearly, because they believe that God does exist, it is better to be in his presence than to be abandoned by him.

Christian understanding of heaven

In complete contrast to hell, Christians believe heaven is being in the eternal presence of God. The Bible describes heaven using many images including those of blinding light, singing and beauty. A good example is contained in Revelation 4. This chapter speaks of 'a rainbow, resembling an emerald' encircling the throne of God. From this throne come 'flashes of lightning, rumblings and peals of thunder'. In front of the throne is what appears to be 'a sea of glass, clear as crystal'. Most Christians take these descriptions as an attempt to show, in a limited way, how perfect and awe-inspiring heaven will be.

Heaven is believed to be a place where suffering and evil no longer exist: 'There will be no more death or mourning or crying or pain' (Revelation 21: 4). A belief in heaven encourages Christians to serve God and be obedient to him. It may also be a comfort in times of suffering. Christians believe that after death this is where they will spend eternity.

The End of Life **57**

Christian understanding of purgatory

Purgatory is a Catholic belief. Catholics believe that if you die in good spiritual state, in friendship with God, you will go to heaven. However, many people are not pure enough to come into God's presence immediately so they undergo PURIFICATION to achieve the holiness necessary to enter into heaven. Catholics call this purgatory, 'the final purification of the elect' (people who will go to heaven), as it is described in the catechism. It is different from the eternal punishment of souls in hell because people in purgatory know that they will go to heaven when they have been purified. This DOCTRINE also explains why Catholics pray for the dead. They do not believe that when you die, you are beyond help; they believe that PRAYERS could help people in purgatory.

The poet only asks to get his head into the heavens. It is the logician who seeks to get the heavens into his head. And it is his head that splits.

G. K. Chesterton, writer (1874–1936)

Because of his transcendence, God cannot be seen as he is, unless he himself opens up his mystery to man's immediate CONTEMPLATION and gives him the capacity for it. The Church calls this contemplation of God in his heavenly glory 'the beatific vision'.

The Catechism of the Catholic Church, 1028

To discuss

Read the two quotes above.

1 What do you think Chesterton means when he says that a poet wants to get his head into heaven?

2 If you were going to write a poem about the Christian idea of heaven, what adjectives would you use?

3 How does the Catechism of the Catholic Church help us to understand what Chesterton meant when he said the logician's head splits when trying to get heaven into his head?

EXAM FOCUS ...

Explain what Christians believe about life after death.

question d), 6 marks

... HINTS

■ This question is asking you to show the different Christian ideas about heaven, hell and purgatory while at the same time showing why Christians hold these beliefs. So you might like to state that purgatory is a Catholic belief which has been taught throughout the ages. Or you might like to say that Christians believe in heaven and hell because this is what the Bible teaches or because of what is said in the Nicene Creed.

■ You might like to refer to the resurrection of Christ as evidence of life after death.

■ You might like to refer to the modern and traditional views of heaven and hell.

Salvation, redemption and the suffering of Christ

Salvation

To receive salvation means to be saved from something. Christian salvation means to be saved from the punishment by God of SIN. Christians believe that God is perfect and that human sin falls short of his standards. In the book of Habakuk in the Bible it says that God can't look upon sin and he cannot tolerate those who do wrong. In Romans the apostle Paul explains sin has to be punished by God. Christians believe that the punishment for sin occurs after death and is called hell.

While a person is on earth, sin destroys their relationship with God as often they choose to live in a way that suggests God does not even exist. For example, they will not obey his commands nor will they worship him.

Christians believe that God is loving and gracious and that he wants to be in relationship with humans. They believe it is because of his great love that he is willing to forgive people of their sin if they ask him for forgiveness and that through repenting of their sinful nature God offers his gift of salvation. His salvation means that the relationship between a person and God is restored so while on earth they can worship him, and he will live in them through the power of the Holy Spirit. After death Christians believe they will be saved from the punishment of hell and given a place in Heaven in the ETERNAL presence of God.

For Christians, salvation means seeking God's forgiveness and following him.

TASKS

1 The photo shows a person walking on the narrow line that is on a broad road. The narrow line represents the way to salvation. Why do you think this is shown using the narrow line rather than the broad road?
2 What does the broad road in the photo represent?
3 What do Christians believe will happen to those who choose the broad road instead of salvation?

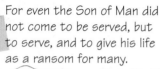

TASKS

4 Explain what Christians mean by the words salvation and redemption.
5 Why was it necessary for Jesus to suffer for human salvation?
6 In what way is Christian salvation a gift?

Bible bitz

For even the Son of Man did not come to be served, but to serve, and to give his life as a ransom for many.

Mark 10: 45

But he was pierced for our transgressions, he was crushed for our iniquities; the punishment that brought us peace was upon him, and by his wounds we are healed.

Isaiah 53: 5

In him we have redemption through his blood, the forgiveness of sins, in accordance with the riches of God's grace.

Ephesians 1: 7

Praise the LORD, O my soul, and forget not all his benefits
who forgives all your sins and heals all your diseases,
who redeems your life from the pit and crowns you with love and compassion

Psalm 103: 2–4

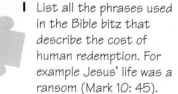

Link it up

1 List all the phrases used in the Bible bitz that describe the cost of human redemption. For example Jesus' life was a ransom (Mark 10: 45).
2 Create a collage or a sketch that helps you to visualise this cost.

Redemption and the suffering of Christ

Christians believe that salvation comes at a price and humans have to be redeemed. To redeem something means to recover ownership of something by paying a sum. Christianity teaches that the cost of human salvation was the death of Jesus. In the Bible in Romans 5: 8 it says 'God demonstrates his own love for us in this: while we were still sinners, Christ died for us' and in the book of Hebrews 9: 28 it says 'so Christ was sacrificed once to take away the sins of many people'.

Christians believe that God placed the punishment for all human disobedience on Jesus when he was crucified. At his death God turned his back on Jesus, Jesus cries out 'my God, my God why have you forsaken me?' (Matthew 27: 46). At this time Christians believe Jesus endured the punishment of God for human sins so that anyone who accepts his SACRIFICE as his or her own no longer stands guilty before God. Jesus' sacrifice was acceptable to God because he, unlike any other human, was himself without sin and not needy of God's forgiveness for himself. Christians believe then that the price for sin has been paid and humans have been redeemed.

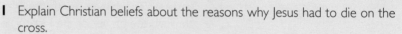

EXAM FOCUS ...

1 Explain Christian beliefs about the reasons why Jesus had to die on the cross.

question d), 6 marks

2 'A forgiving God would not send people to hell.'
Discuss this statement. You should include different, supported points of view and a personal viewpoint. You must refer to Christianity in your answer.

question e), 12 marks

... HINTS

Question 1
■ Your answer would need to relate the story of the passion of Jesus (his suffering and death) to Christian ideas of salvation and redemption. Try to use these terms and explain them in your own words to show the examiner the full depth of your understanding.
■ You could link the ideas to biblical quotes – see the Bible bitz on the left.

Question 2
■ Remember – it is important to show different points of view and also your own personal point of view.
■ This question is asking you to discuss and evaluate (look at the arguments for and against) and then come to a conclusion on whether the statement is true or false. You may not want to agree or disagree entirely – that is fine but you must support your conclusion with a valid reason.
■ You could agree with the statement by referring to Christian beliefs that God is forgiving and link this idea to Christian/biblical teachings such as the parable of the prodigal son (Luke 15: 11–32).
■ You could agree by relating your answer to the Christian beliefs of why God appeared as Jesus (John 3: 16) and why Jesus had to suffer and die in such a way.
■ You could then discuss the concept of hell and ask the question why God would create such a place.
■ Remember to include your opinion as a conclusion and support it.

'God Will Be My Judge'

Updated: 22:24, Saturday March 04, 2006

Tony Blair has provoked a furious row about comments he made about his FAITH.

The Prime Minister said God would be the ultimate judge of his decision to send troops to Iraq.

In an interview with veteran broadcaster Michael Parkinson, he also hinted his decisions are God's as well.

Mr Blair said of the Iraq invasion: 'I think if you have faith about these things then you realise that judgment is made by other people.'

Asked to explain what he meant, Mr Blair replied: 'If you believe in God, it's made by God as well.'

His comments echo those of President Bush, who reportedly claimed last year that his decision to invade Iraq was a 'mission from God'.

Mr Blair's comments have been fiercely criticised by the families of troops killed in Iraq.

Anti-war campaigner Rose Gentle, whose son Gordon was killed in Basra in 2004, said: 'A good Christian wouldn't be for this war. I'm actually quite disgusted.'

Liberal Democrat MP Dr Evan Harris said: 'Our political system relies on decisions being made by accountable and elected politicians, not by their, or anyone else's, Gods.

'It is a bizarre and shocking revelation that the Prime Minister claims to have been guided by the SUPERNATURAL in this matter.'

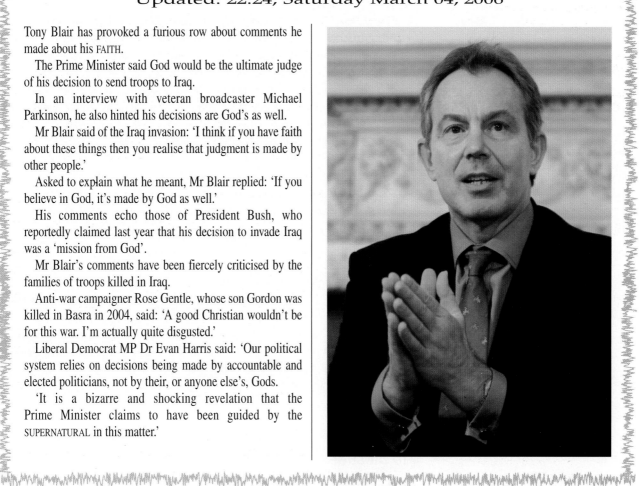

To discuss

1 What do you think former Prime Minister Tony Blair meant when he said that God would be his ultimate judge?

2 How do you think judgement by God and judgement by human beings is different? You could think about:

- the type of punishment or reward each has the power to give
- the length any punishment or reward might last
- the standards by which God would judge compared to the standards by which another human might judge.

3 Select from the list below the three most important characteristics that a good judge should have. Explain why you have chosen each characteristic.

Fair	Honest	Unprejudiced	A good listener
	Moral	Forgiving	

God as judge

Christians believe that God is the ultimate judge of all humankind. They believe that at death God will judge all people according to both their faith in him and their actions. God's nature means that Christians believe him to be the perfect judge, possessing all the qualities required to make the right judgement, qualities that we hope to see in our law court judges.

Dilys

When I think about God, I have to remind myself that my human understanding is very limited. I can often get things wrong when I try to understand the people and events I deal with each day. So when I try to understand the God who has created me and holds me in being, it's not surprising that my mind finds it a bit of a struggle. I then remember that God, the God 'whose power, working in us, can do infinitely more than we can ask or imagine' (Ephesians 3: 20) loves me with an everlasting love.

When I see my own weakness and failings, I worry that I am not living up to what God expects of me. Then, sooner or later, God stops me thinking of myself – by the word of a friend, by the beauty of the song of a blackbird, by someone in need – and I am set free to love again.

As I am drawn on by this amazing love, I have come to see that the concept of God as judge often provokes fear, and that fear is the opposite of love, because fear makes us retreat into ourselves. That is not to say that we are not judged by God – but God is love, so we are judged by love, and we are judged on how we have loved. And the love that judges us is the love that has created us and redeemed us, so there is no need to be afraid.

To discuss

4 Dilys speaks of the concept of God as a judge provoking fear. Why do you think that some people have a sense of fear when considering God as judge?

5 Does Dilys' explanation of her belief in a God that is love help to remove this sense of fear?

6 What do you think Christians believe 'God's expectations' are? Do you think anyone can live up to them?

The Sheep and the Goats (Matthew 25)

When the Son of Man comes in his glory, and all the angels with him, he will sit on his throne in heavenly glory. All the nations will be gathered before him, and he will separate the people one from another as a shepherd separates the sheep from the goats. He will put the sheep on his right and the goats on his left.

Then the King will say to those on his right, 'Come, you who are blessed by my Father; take your inheritance, the kingdom prepared for you since the creation of the world. For I was hungry and you gave me something to eat, I was thirsty and you gave me something to drink, I was a stranger and you invited me in, I needed clothes and you clothed me, I was sick and you looked after me, I was in prison and you came to visit me.'

Then the righteous will answer him, 'Lord, when did we see you hungry and feed you, or thirsty and give you something to drink? When did we see you a stranger and invite you in, or needing clothes and clothe you? When did we see you sick or in prison and go to visit you?'

The King will reply, 'I tell you the truth, whatever you did for one of the least of these brothers of mine, you did for me.'

Then he will say to those on his left, 'Depart from me, you who are cursed, into the eternal fire prepared for the devil and his angels. For I was hungry and you gave me nothing to eat, I was thirsty and you gave me nothing to drink, I was a stranger and you did not invite me in, I needed clothes and you did not clothe me, I was sick and in prison and you did not look after me.'

They also will answer, 'Lord, when did we see you hungry or thirsty or a stranger or needing clothes or sick or in prison, and did not help you?'

He will reply, 'I tell you the truth, whatever you did not do for one of the least of these, you did not do for me.'

Then they will go away to eternal punishment, but the righteous to eternal life.

Link it up

Humankind is divided into two groups in the Sheep and Goats PARABLE about judgement.

1 What type of people are represented by the goats? Explain how you know this.

2 What type of people are represented by the sheep? Explain how you know this.

3 According to this parable, who is responsible for how a person is judged by God?

4 Based on this parable, how do you think a Christian believes that they should live their life? Support your answer with quotes from the parable.

5 What effect do you think this parable might have on the way a person chooses to live their life?

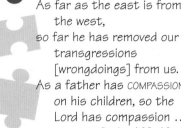

Repentance and forgiveness

The PARABLE of the sheep and the goats (see page 63) teaches Christians that humans will be judged and then punished or rewarded eternally. Christians do not believe that they will be sent to eternal punishment if they fail to do right all the time. They believe God to be loving and forgiving. Through their CONFESSION and repentance he removes their wrongdoings so they can no longer be found guilty for them (1 John 1: 9). Jesus' death is believed to have been the punishment required by God for the wrongdoings of humankind. God's law does not require any further punishment for human SIN.

Christians believe that the judgement they receive after death depends on their behaviour and their faith in God during life. This belief should encourage people to live morally, according to the laws of God. People should recognise when they do wrong and confess it to God, with the intention of not doing the same thing again. They should trust God to help them live in the way that he wants them to.

STRETCH WHAT YOU KNOW

1 Romans 8: 1–2 says that for Christians there is no condemnation because they are free from their sin. Using the other Bible quotes, explain:

- ■ what Christians believe they are no longer condemned to
- ■ why they believe they are no longer condemned.

2 Explain why you think the writer of Psalm 103 described God, the judge, as compassionate.

EXAM FOCUS …

'If you behave badly in this life you will be punished after you die.'

Discuss this statement. You should include different, supported points of view and a personal viewpoint. You must refer to Christianity in your answer.

question e), 12 marks

… HINTS

- ■ Remember – it is important to show different points of view and also your own personal point of view.
- ■ This question is asking you to discuss and evaluate (look at the arguments for and against) and then come to a conclusion on whether the statement is true or false. You may not want to agree or disagree entirely – that is fine but you must support your conclusion with a valid reason.
- ■ You might like to begin your answer by showing the Christian belief in God as Judge and supporting this with reference to the parable of the sheep and the goats. However, in contrast you could discuss the Christian idea of forgiveness and repentance using for support the parable of the prodigal son.
- ■ You might like to include an atheist point of view.
- ■ Remember to include your own point of view.

Christian funeral rites, and the ways in which these reflect belief and aim to support the bereaved

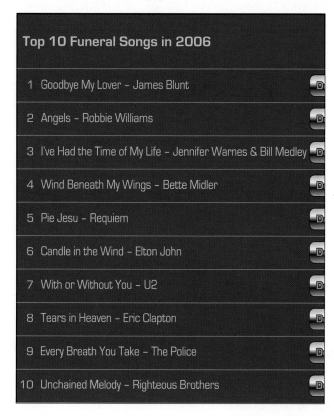

Top 10 Funeral Songs in 2006

1 Goodbye My Lover – James Blunt

2 Angels – Robbie Williams

3 I've Had the Time of My Life – Jennifer Warnes & Bill Medley

4 Wind Beneath My Wings – Bette Midler

5 Pie Jesu – Requiem

6 Candle in the Wind – Elton John

7 With or Without You – U2

8 Tears in Heaven – Eric Clapton

9 Every Breath You Take – The Police

10 Unchained Melody – Righteous Brothers

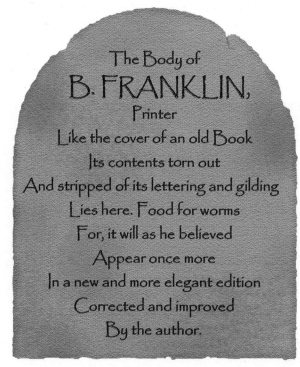

The Body of
B. FRANKLIN,
Printer
Like the cover of an old Book
Its contents torn out
And stripped of its lettering and gilding
Lies here. Food for worms
For, it will as he believed
Appear once more
In a new and more elegant edition
Corrected and improved
By the author.

Benjamin Franklin, a Founding Father of the United States, wrote this epitaph for himself as a young man

To discuss

1 Look at the titles of the top ten songs above. You may already be familiar with the lyrics to some of them. What reasons do you think people may have for choosing these songs for their funerals?

2 What songs would you place in a top ten list for funerals? Why?

3 The only Christian song in the top ten is 'Pie Jesu'. Why do you think there are not more traditional Christian hymns in this list?

TASKS

An EPITAPH gives honour to someone who has died and is usually inscribed on their tombstone.

1 Explain what Franklin's epitaph means and how it reflects the Christian understanding of death.

2 What do you think would be the best epitaph that anyone could hope for? Explain your answer.

3 Do you think epitaphs are worth having? Why?

Many people will, at some point in their life, consider their own death and how they would like to be remembered. Some people even plan their own funerals, including the music, to ensure their life is celebrated in the way they want. A funeral marks the close of a human life on earth but for Christians it also serves as a reminder of the hope of an afterlife with God. A Christian funeral service thanks God for the dead person's life on earth, celebrating it as an act of love. The mourners might benefit from attending the funeral service in several ways.

■ It is an acknowledgement that the person is no longer part of this world but safe in God's care.

■ They can draw comfort from other mourners, and in the reassurance that the dead person lives on with God.

■ They might feel happiness as the dead person's life is celebrated.

■ It is an opportunity to express publicly their love or admiration for the dead person.

■ It marks the beginning of a life without the person who has died, in which the loved one is remembered.

A Christian funeral service

Funeral services vary slightly between denominations, but there are some common features.

Bible reading – the reading focuses on the prospect of eternal life with God after death. For example, 'I am the resurrection and the life. He who believes in me will live, even though he dies.' (John 11: 25)

EULOGY – this is a talk or speech in which the person's life is remembered and their achievements are acknowledged, often through the sharing of memories. Close friends or relatives usually contribute to this aspect of the service. The minister will also remind the CONGREGATION of the Christian beliefs about life and death.

Prayers – prayers are said for the friends and relatives of the dead person, asking God to support them in their time of grief, and that they may have strength to move on. The dead person is entrusted to the care of God. In a Catholic service prayers will also be said for the dead person.

Hymns – one or more hymns might be sung. As with the Bible reading the focus is likely to be on the hope of an afterlife with God. Sometimes the hymns are those chosen before their death by the person who has died, or they may be favourites of the dead person, chosen by relatives and friends.

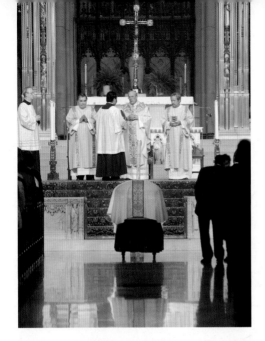

Holy Communion – in Catholic funerals MASS is almost always performed, and it is not uncommon in other denominations either. It reminds the mourners of the death and resurrection of Christ, which has provided for humankind the possibility of eternal life with God.

The dead person might then be buried in the ground, or they might be cremated. At the graveside it is usual for further prayers to be said before the final COMMITTAL STATEMENT by the minister. The committal statement is also said at a CREMATION as the curtain shuts around the coffin. The wording of the committal varies between denominations; this is the Church of England one: 'We therefore commit his (or her) body to the ground; earth to earth, ashes to ashes, dust to dust; in sure and certain hope of the Resurrection to eternal life.'

STRETCH WHAT YOU KNOW

Some people consider the impact on the environment when planning a funeral. It is now possible to have environmentally friendly funerals where the coffins are biodegradable and the burial takes place in an area of woodland.

1   Go to www.funeralsearch.co.uk/woodlands.php and find out about:

- green or eco coffins
- woodland or green burials
- tree planting.

2   Do you think that an environmentally friendly funeral would reflect the Christian concepts of stewardship (see page 112)? Explain your answer.

Link it up

1   How is the Christian belief about eternal life after death reflected in their funeral services?

2   Explain whether you think that a Christian funeral service is helpful to mourners.

EXAM FOCUS ...

Explain how a Christian funeral service might help comfort the relative of someone who has died.

question d), 6 marks

... HINTS

- This question is asking you to show how the symbols, actions and words used in a Christian funeral service help to show that there is life after death and therefore this would comfort a relative.
- So you might like to discuss the flowers; the eulogy; the words used by the vicar/priest at the beginning of the service (John 11: 25) and the words said by the graveside.

LET'S REVISE

Christian understanding of the relationship between the body and the soul

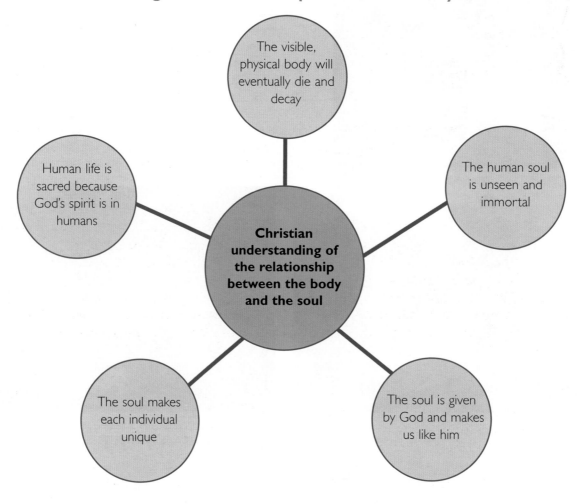

The visible, physical body will eventually die and decay

The human soul is unseen and immortal

Human life is sacred because God's spirit is in humans

Christian understanding of the relationship between the body and the soul

The soul makes each individual unique

The soul is given by God and makes us like him

TASKS

4 Write five statements about Christian understanding of the relationship between the body and the soul. Make some of your statements true and some false. Use the revision diagram and the information on page 54 to help you.

■ Swap your statements with someone else in your class.
■ Identify which of their statements are true and which are false.
■ Correct the false statements.
■ Give the statements back to the person who wrote them and see if they have identified and corrected your false statements.

5 Create your own revision cards on the topic of The End of Life. Include:

■ hell
■ heaven
■ purgatory
■ the concept of God as judge
■ funeral rites.

LET'S **RE**VISE

Exam focus

a) What is purgatory?   *1 mark*
- This question requires you to give a brief explanation of the Catholic belief in a place where souls go to be cleansed before they can enter heaven.

b) What is meant by the word 'salvation'?   *2 marks*
- This question is asking you to show your understanding of the word 'salvation'. You could state that 'it is the act of the soul being saved through the death of Jesus Christ'.

c) What do Christians believe about the soul?   *3 marks*
- Your responses to this question could focus on how Adam was created and that the soul is the spiritual aspect of the person whilst the body is the material part which returns to dust at the end of life.
- You could respond by showing that some Christians think it is the soul only which returns to heaven and that St Paul stated we receive a new spiritual body (1 Corinthians 15) while other Christians believe it is the body and soul which go to heaven and thus cremation is not allowed.

d) Explain how a Christian funeral service reflects beliefs about the end of life.   *6 marks*
- Your answer could include the words stated in the service by the vicar such as at the opening of the service when he or she says: 'I am the resurrection and the life', which reflect Christian beliefs of life in heaven for the believer.
- Your answer could include the symbols seen in a funeral service such as the empty cross; the flowers and the candles. You will need to explain what these symbols represent.
- Your answer could refer to the belief of the resurrection of Christ.

e) 'This life is more important than the next.'
Discuss this statement. You should include different, supported points of view and a personal viewpoint. You must refer to Christianity in your answer.   *12 marks*
- Remember – it is important to show different points of view and also your own personal point of view.
- This question is asking you to discuss and evaluate (look at the arguments for and against) and then come to a conclusion on whether the statement is true or false. You may not want to agree or disagree entirely – that is fine but you must support your conclusion with a valid reason.
- Your answer could refer to the fact that this life is important because it is preparation for life in heaven.
- You could show a secular view that this life is the only life and therefore it is very important.
- You could refer to the fact that for a Christian life in heaven is the ultimate goal and thus is the most important.
- Remember to give your own viewpoint and support it.

TOPIC 4

Good and Evil

Key Concepts

In this topic you will learn about:

- Christian beliefs about good and evil
- The problem of evil
- Christian approaches to why there is evil and suffering in the world
- Christian responses to the problem of evil
- Coping with suffering
- Sources and reasons for moral behaviour.

Christians believe that God is both all powerful and all loving. They also believe in the existence of the Devil in some form. The Devil desires to work against God and is a force for evil. Christians aim to obey God and avoid evil. By doing this, they believe that they will be rewarded after death. In order to understand exactly how God wants them to live, Christians read their Bibles, consider the example of the life of Christ and listen to their conscience. At times when they are tested through suffering or difficulty, they gain strength through their FAITH, seeking God in PRAYER and trusting him to guide their lives.

Christian beliefs about good and evil

Christians believe that God is perfect and the source of all goodness. They believe that humans were created in his likeness and have responsibility to live in a way that is pleasing to him. The moral code given by God in the Bible is what Christians follow to live a good life. Evil is the result of not following God. Augustine (354–430CE) taught that evil was the act of turning away from the ultimate goodness of God. In Christianity evil is often personified in the character of the devil. The devil acts against God and wants to tempt humans to behave in the same evil way. For example, in Genesis the devil, in the form of a serpent, tempted Eve to eat the fruit forbidden to her by God.

God and the Devil

> ## To discuss
>
> 1 Identify the cartoon character on the left.
>
> 2 How do you recognise this character?
>
> 3 Why do you think some people believe in the existence of the Devil as a real creature?

The Screwtape Letters

The Screwtape Letters is a book written by C. S. Lewis, the author of the Narnia stories. The story takes the form of a series of letters from a senior devil to a lesser devil, Wormwood, advising him on how to make a Christian man, known as 'the Patient', disobedient to God.

> My dear Wormwood,
>
> I note with grave displeasure that your patient has become a Christian. Do not indulge the hope that you will escape the usual penalties ... In the meantime we must make the best of the situation. There is no need to despair; hundreds of these adult converts have been reclaimed after a brief stay in the Enemy's camp and are now with us. All the habits of the patient, both mental and bodily, are still in our favour.
>
> Chapter 2, page 15

> My dear Wormwood,
>
> I wonder you should ask me whether it is essential to keep the patient in ignorance of your own existence ... Our policy, for the moment, is to conceal ourselves ... I do not think you will have much difficulty in keeping your patient in the dark. The fact that devils are predominantly comic figures in the modern imagination will help you. If any faint suspicion of your existence begins to arise in his mind, suggest to him a picture of something in red tights, and persuade him that since he cannot believe in that he therefore cannot believe in you.
>
> Chapter 7, page 39

> My dear Wormwood,
>
> I note with great displeasure that the Enemy has, for the time being, put a forcible end to your direct attacks on the patient. You ought to have known that he always does in the end, and you ought to have stopped before you reached that stage. For as things are, your man has discovered the dangerous truth that these attacks don't last forever ...
>
> Chapter 20, page 101

TASKS

1 Who do you think is the enemy referred to in *The Screwtape Letters*?
2 Why does the senior devil suggest that Wormwood allows his patient to think of him as a character in red tights?
3 How believable do you find the existence of the traditional red, horned creature that is used to portray the Devil?
4 From the extracts you have read, whom do you think C. S. Lewis considers to be most powerful – God or the Devil?

C. S. Lewis's book *The Screwtape Letters* builds on the character of the Devil that is outlined in the Bible. He makes the Devil and his understudies real creatures, which reflects the traditional view. The Devil is traditionally shown as a red creature with horns, holding a pitchfork. He is also known by other names, including Satan and Lucifer. It is this creature that some people blame for all the suffering in the world.

However, not all Christians believe in the Devil as a real being. Some believe the Devil is a symbolic way of showing how people often struggle to do what is right, and that there is always the temptation to do things that are wrong. For some Christians the battle that they experience within themselves to do what is right is what they understand to be the work of the Devil – 'he' is an evil force, not a real being.

The Devil in the Bible

Other Christians believe the Devil is a real being, as portrayed in the Bible. In the Bible it says that the Devil was originally a good angel created by God. However, he tried to make himself better than God and for this reason God threw him out of heaven. The Devil has limited power and tries to persuade humans to be disobedient to God in the same way that he is. This is seen in Genesis 3 when he disguises himself as a serpent and convinces Eve to eat the fruit that God told her she must not eat.

For Satan himself masquerades as an angel of light.

2 Corinthians 11: 14

When the Pharisees heard this, they said 'It is only by Beelzebub, the prince of demons, that this fellow [Jesus] drives out demons.'

Matthew 12: 24

Your enemy the devil prowls around like a roaring lion looking for someone to devour.

1 Peter 5: 8

The great dragon was hurled down – that ancient serpent called the devil, or Satan, who leads the whole world astray.

Revelation 12: 9

I saw Satan fall like lightning from heaven.

Luke 10: 18

The Devil is also present in the story of Job. Job is a man who is obedient to God, but the Devil suggests to God that Job is only obedient to him because God protects him and looks after him so well. God therefore allows the Devil to bring all kinds of suffering upon Job to see whether he will continue to be faithful to God. Job does remain faithful and God rewards him.

Jesus is also tempted to be disobedient to God by the Devil just after his baptism. While Jesus is in the desert Satan offers him food, wealth and power (Luke 4: 8), but, just like Job, Jesus remains faithful to God.

Christians believe that God has destroyed the Devil and his work, and that he is bound to hell for eternity (1 John 3: 8). God, as the creator of all things, is all powerful, is loving, compassionate, forgiving and faithful (Exodus 34: 6). The Devil therefore has limited power and his power will eventually be brought to an end by God.

> Scripture speaks of a SIN of these angels. This 'fall' consists in the free choice of these created spirits, who radically [extremely] and irrevocably [unalterably] rejected God and his reign. We find a reflection of that rebellion in the tempter's word to our first parents: 'You will be like God.' The devil 'has sinned from the beginning', he is 'a liar and the father of lies'.
>
> *Catechism of the Catholic Church, 392*

Link it up

1 List the different ways that the Devil is described in the Bible quotes above.

2 How does the character you have just described compare to the Christian understanding of God as described in the text above?

STRETCH **WHAT YOU KNOW**

1 Compare the Devil's desire to be like God to the account in Genesis 3 of Eve taking and eating the forbidden fruit. In what way are the two events similar in outcome?

2 Read the extract above from the Catechism of the Catholic Church. The text mentions that the free choice (or free will) that angels and humans have has led to disobedience. Disobedience to God has ultimately resulted in suffering. Do you think it would have been better for God never to have given humans free will? Explain your answer.

EXAM FOCUS ...

Explain Christian beliefs about the Devil (Satan).

question d), 6 marks

... HINTS

■ You could begin your answer by giving a traditional view of the devil and perhaps support this with the idea that this image came about in medieval times as a way for the Church to encourage people to listen to the word of God.

■ You could support the idea of the Devil existing by referring to the occasions he is mentioned in the Bible.

■ You could include a more modern view of the Devil as a symbol of evil rather than an existing being.

To discuss

1 Adam and Eve are at the forefront of the picture by Gustave Doré. Where do you think they are going? Why?

2 In the background behind the angel there are shafts of light compared to the darkness at the front of the picture. What do you think this contrast of light represents?

3 Explain what Christians believe the effect of Adam and Eve's original sin was on the rest of humanity.

4 How does redemption by God affect the way a Christian chooses to live.

The Fall, original sin and redemption

Christians believe that at creation Adam and Eve were in a state of innocence and in a perfect relationship with God (Genesis 1–3). In the Garden of Eden God forbade Adam and Eve to eat from the tree which would give them knowledge of good and evil. Eve was tempted by the serpent to disobey God and eat the fruit, Adam also shared in the fruit. Aware of their own nakedness and having lost their innocence they are banished from the garden by God. The Fall is the phrase Christians use to describe this move of humans from a perfect relationship with God to disobedience and a broken relationship.

Many Christians believe that the Fall has affected the entire human race. They believe that every person born since the Fall is affected by this original sin. Christians believe that original sin means that all humans are born out of relationship with God and in need of his salvation (see page 59). Original sin means that without redemption a person has no hope of ETERNAL life in Heaven with God.

Christians believe that redemption is God's plan for restoring humans to a relationship with him and that people who choose to seek God's forgiveness will have their relationship with God restored. Jesus' death on the cross acts as the substitute for the punishment that their original sin deserved. Christians believe that having been forgiven they should then aim to live according to God's commands and in his will. However, Christians believe that humans who choose to live out of relationship with God and in disobedience to him will be punished – at death they will be condemned to hell.

Adam and Eve banished from the Garden of Eden, an engraving by Gustave Doré (1832–83), 1865.

The problem of evil

Evil is often divided into two categories, natural evil and moral evil. Natural evil is suffering created through no direct fault of humans. This includes all natural disasters, such as earthquakes and tornadoes that bring devastation and tragedy to innocent people. Moral evil is when suffering is caused by the actions of human beings. For example, when Adolf Hitler tried to kill the entire Jewish race in Europe in the 1930s and 1940s he caused immeasurable suffering.

The fact of suffering undoubtedly constitutes the single greatest challenge to the Christian faith.

John Stott, Christian writer and Anglican minister (1921–)

To discuss

1 Why do you think John Stott identifies suffering as the greatest challenge facing Christians?

2 What other problems do you think Christianity faces? Do you think any of these is greater than the problem of suffering? Use the ideas below to help you to respond to this.

- Increased interest in other religions including Islam and Buddhism.
- Declining church attendance.
- Negative attitudes towards Christianity.
- Changing attitudes in society – for example, whether couples should get married before having children.

TASKS

1 Identify what is happening in photos A–F on page 75 (answers on page 119).
2 List the main causes for each event.
3 Do you think God has any responsibility for any of the events shown in the photos?
4 Divide the events shown in photos A–F into two groups, moral evil and natural evil.
5 Do you think humans bear greatest responsibility for either of these types of evil, or do you think God or the Devil is to blame for all evil? Give reasons for your answer.
6 What could humans do to reduce suffering?
7 At times of disaster people often ask the question 'Why do innocent people suffer?' What questions would you like to ask God about suffering and evil in our world?

Christian approaches to why there is evil and suffering in the world

TASKS

1 In what way do Augustine and Iranaeus differ in their view of the Genesis story of the Fall?

2 Explain the beliefs Christians have about the reason for suffering.

3 Explain what you think are the most convincing reasons for evil and suffering in the world.

Christians have different views on why there is suffering in the world. In the Genesis story of the FALL, evil first disrupts a perfect world when Eve disobeys God. Adam and Eve both use the freedom that God has given them to do what he has commanded them not to do. Not only is the perfect world affected but so is the perfect relationship that humans originally had with God. This account led St Augustine, a Christian monk (354–430CE), to teach that evil is the sole responsibility of human beings for making wrong choices. Often, this view leaves people asking why God chose to create Adam and Eve if he knew they were going to be disobedient.

However, Iranaeus, also a Christian monk (130–202CE), suggested a different view of this story in Genesis. Iranaeus suggested that man was not created perfect but immature, needing to grow and develop to perfection, as planned by God. Evil is part of the process towards becoming more like God. So some Christians believe that evil is necessary for us to understand goodness. If there was no wrongdoing then we would be unaware of justice. It is because of the existence of evil that we can be aware of the goodness of God. From this perspective the existence of evil teaches us lessons.

This notion, however, does not explain suffering that cannot be learned from, for example, the suffering of a baby. Sometimes suffering does not help us to develop God's perfect qualities and become more like him; it is then hard to see why it is necessary. For example, when a person is diagnosed with a terminal illness they may feel that they do not deserve the illness. They may feel a sense of anger towards God for allowing them to be ill, especially if they believe that they have tried to live in a way that would please God.

Other Christians think that suffering is a test of FAITH for believers and a punishment for the wicked. In the book of Job God allows the Devil to bring evil and suffering on Job to see whether he will remain faithful to God. Job does remain faithful and God rewards him. Some Christians may believe that they too have been tested by God during difficult times in their lives, trusting that he will never allow them to be tested beyond what they can bear (1 Corinthians 10: 13).

STRETCH WHAT YOU KNOW

Read the following extract from the New Advent Catholic website:

'St Thomas Aquinas, a thirteenth-century Christian monk, provides an explanation of why God chose to create anything at all. First, it is asked why God, foreseeing that his creatures would use the gift of free will for their own injury, did not either abstain from creating them, or in some way safeguard their free will from misuse, or else deny them the gift altogether? St Thomas replies that God cannot change His mind, since the Divine will is free from the defect of weakness or MUTABILITY. Such mutability would, it should be remarked, be a defect in the Divine nature (and therefore impossible), because if God's purpose were made dependent on the foreseen free act of any creature, God would thereby SACRIFICE His own freedom, and would submit Himself to His creatures, thus ABDICATING His essential SUPREMACY.'

1 Why does Aquinas say that God continued to create Adam and Eve even though he knew they would disobey him?

2 Explain what you think would be the effect of a God who abdicated his supremacy.

Christian responses to the problem of evil

Christians have to bring together their belief in an all powerful and all loving God with their experience of life which includes evil and suffering.

St Augustine believed that evil was spoiled goodness. Augustine taught that evil is the act of a person freely turning away from all that is from God and is therefore good. Evil and suffering are therefore the result of human free will. This does not conflict with God being all loving nor does it suggest he lacks power. In this explanation God chooses to co-exist with evil for a period of time as he allows humans to exercise the free will that he has given to them.

A cartoonist's take on what happened to Adam and Eve.

TASKS

1 Look at the cartoon above. How does this suggest the first act of disobedience against God occurred?
2 If Eve disobeyed God by eating some of the forbidden fruit at the serpent's suggestion, who do you think is responsible – Eve or the serpent?
3 Read the story of Adam, Eve and the serpent in Genesis 3. Explain whom God punishes for this first act of evil, and how.

Keith

The existence of evil is a tough question with no simple answers, but that does not mean there are no answers at all. My response involves both faith and logic. Faith, in the Bible as God's inspired word, and logic in making sense of what the Bible says.

Evil comes from the freedom that God, in his love, put into the universe. Freedom is an essential aspect of love as love cannot be compelled, but freedom involves the ability to choose not to respond to God in love and obedience. Evil comes from two such choices – that of Lucifer (Satan) and that of human beings – to reject God and choose an independent destiny.

These decisions have affected our world in many ways. Some evil is a direct or indirect result of the activities of Satan in and through people's lives. Some evil is a direct or indirect result of human activity. Some evil appears to be the result of natural occurrences (such as earthquakes, disease and drought). According to the Bible, mankind's choice to ignore God (sin) affected the whole of creation negatively and the planet does not function as originally intended by God.

What helps me cope with evil and suffering is knowing what God has done to deal with these causes of evil. Out of his love for us, he entered this world to experience and deal with evil first-hand. He knows what it is like to suffer the effects of evil. Through his death on the cross, Jesus defeated the power of Satan; through his RESURRECTION he defeated death (the ultimate result of evil) and he lives to open a way for people to be reconciled to the God they had turned away from. Through his Spirit he offers the power to change human nature, to forgive when hurt, to love when hated. He promises to return to end this broken world and create a new heaven and a new earth, which will be my permanent home.

EXAM FOCUS ...

'If people suffer, it is usually their own fault.'

Discuss this statement. You should include different, supported points of view and a personal viewpoint. You must refer to Christianity in your answer.

question e), 12 marks

To discuss

1   What does Keith identify as the reason for Christ coming to earth, dying and returning to life?

2   How do you think that knowing Jesus has experienced the effects of evil is a help to Christians?

3   Keith says that God's Spirit offers the power to change human nature, but he also says that humans are free to reject this. If this is true do you think there will ever be an end to moral evil on earth? Give reasons for your answer.

... HINTS

■   Remember – it is important to show different points of view and also your own personal point of view.
■   This question is asking you to discuss and evaluate (look at the arguments for and against) and then come to a conclusion on whether the statement is true or false. You may not want to agree or disagree entirely – that is fine but you must support your conclusion with a valid reason.
■   Your answer could refer to the difference between moral and natural evil, which lead to suffering, linking moral evil to the concept of free will and the example of Adam and Eve disobeying God.
■   You could link the idea of people suffering to the example of Job in the Old Testament and also to other ideas as to why it may be necessary to allow evil and suffering in this world.
■   You could give examples of people suffering when it is not their fault.
■   Remember to include your own view and support it.

Coping with suffering

To discuss

1 In his prayer what does St Ignatius ask God for and why?

2 How do you think Christians believe that prayer can help them in their suffering?

Father, make us more like Jesus.
Help us to bear difficulty, pain, disappointment and sorrows,
knowing that in your perfect working and design you can use such bitter
experiences to shape our characters and make us more like our Lord.
We look with hope for that day when we shall be wholly like Christ,
because we shall see him as he is.
AMEN.

Prayer by St Ignatius, before his martyrdom in 107CE

Christian beliefs about suffering

There are many reasons for suffering in the world but one thing is certain – people do suffer. Christians believe that God is loving and compassionate, that he is aware of human suffering and cares about how people feel.

Christians speak to God in prayer, in the belief that he hears them and will comfort and strengthen them in their suffering. Christians may also pray for God's intervention in their situation – for example, that God will heal them from an illness. Christians believe that God will answer prayer, but whether he does what is asked for in the prayer or not depends on whether it is his will also.

Christians believe that in all situations God has a plan that is in the best interests of humankind, even though humans are unaware of his plan and may be conscious only of the immense suffering they are going through. God works through all situations to bring about good. This may mean a person with an illness is healed but it may be that they continue to suffer or die. Either way, Christians believe God is caring for the people involved. For example, by continuing to suffer, a person's FAITH may be growing and bringing them closer to God, or they may be giving encouragement to others who are suffering. So by not healing them, God can still be working out the best plan.

Christians believe that God is able to understand and relate to human suffering because Jesus himself came to earth and suffered. In this way the Bible teaches that humans share in the suffering of Christ and he in our suffering. Jesus was whipped and crucified; he died an agonising death despite asking God if it was possible to not go through with such pain (Luke 22: 42). Times of suffering have made many Christians feel closer to God, as they learn to rely on him for strength and support. Christians aim to trust God and to accept that whatever is happening in their lives is in the care of God.

Cast all your anxiety on him because he cares for you.

1 Peter 5: 7

Is any one of you sick? He should call the elders of the church to pray over him and anoint him with oil … the prayer of a righteous man is powerful and effective.

James 5: 14 and 16

And pray in the Spirit on all occasions with all kinds of prayers and requests.

Ephesians 6: 18

This is the confidence we have in approaching God: that if we ask anything according to his will, he hears us. And if we know he hears us – whatever we ask – we know that we have what we ask of him.

1 John 5: 14–15

… then we are heirs – heirs of God and co-heirs with Christ, if indeed we share in his sufferings in order that we may also share in his glory.

Romans 8: 17

For just as the sufferings of Christ flow over into our lives, so also through Christ our comfort overflows.

2 Corinthians 1: 5

Jesus prayed, 'Father, if you are willing, take this cup from me; yet not my will, but yours be done.'

Luke 22: 42

Look carefully at this picture: is there more than one way of seeing it? Do you immediately notice the different ways it could be seen?

To discuss

3 Describe what the picture above seemed to be of when you first looked at it.

4 Explain how the image changes when you spend more time looking at it.

5 How can this picture be used as an ANALOGY to what Christians believe about God's view of the world compared to our human view?

6 Can you identify any examples of suffering in our world where Christians might struggle to see God's good big picture?

Mark

The Bible says that weeping lasts for the night but joy comes in the morning. This verse sums up for me how praying to God can help one cope with suffering. Of course we may struggle with suffering, but beyond that suffering God promises us joy. This may be joy on earth as we overcome the suffering or joy in heaven when we die and spend eternity with him. When a close relative died I prayed to God to help me overcome my grief. The experience of prayer had a healing quality that I could really sense, where God's love penetrated my hurt and nurtured me into an acceptance of any given difficulty. Therefore I, like many people the world over, have a knowledge and experience that joy truly does come after suffering when you rely on God through prayer.

TASKS

1 Mark says that God can bring joy after suffering because the suffering lasts only for a time. In your own experience do you think this is true?
2 Do you think Mark is right to accept suffering without questioning God?

Link it up

1 From the Bible quotes on page 80 opposite identify:
   - when Christians should pray
   - how Christians should pray
   - why Christians should pray.

2 In 1 John 5 it says that prayer requests will be fulfilled according to God's will. How does this help us to understand why some prayer requests are not fulfilled in the way we would want them to be?

3 How did Jesus suffer?

4 According to the Bible quotes, what is the link between the suffering of Jesus and other human suffering? Use the bullet points below to help you start to construct an answer:
   - Jesus suffered and so do humans.
   - Jesus can comfort humans.
   - Humans will share Jesus' glory.

EXAM FOCUS ...

Explain how a Christian may cope with suffering.

question d), 6 marks

... HINTS

- This question can be answered in two ways (or both!). You could answer it by explaining Christian ideas on why God allows suffering to happen, and that this would then allow Christians to have a better understanding of why it was happening and they would be able to cope with all the problems.
- Or you might like to address it by giving Christian responses (what they would do) if they were faced with their own or other people's suffering. So you could give the examples of prayer, reading the Bible and charity. But you must not just list or describe what they would do; you must also explain why these actions are important and attempt to link them to specific Bible or Christian teachings.
- You may like to refer to the different ways of suffering: physical, mental, religious and emotional.

Sources and reasons for moral behaviour

Read the questions below and choose an answer A), B) or C). Keep a record of your answers and see what your result is at the end.

1 **Your friend has bought a new outfit for a party. It looks hideous but they think that they are the hottest thing on this earth. What do you do?**

A) Tell them the truth, they'll only make a fool of themselves if you don't.

B) Suggest that the world isn't ready for such class yet and that they shouldn't waste such a great outfit on such a small party, hope they fall for it and choose to wear something different.

C) Tell them they look great – after all, they've got eyes, haven't they, and if they can't see the problem that's not your fault is it? Besides, they'll make you look better!

2 **You find £20 on the path outside your house when you leave for school one morning. What do you do?**

A) Pick it up and take it to the police – if no one claims it then the police have your details and can pass it back to you anyway.

B) Take the £20 and promise yourself that you will donate half of it to a charity. Keep the other half as a reward for finding it in the first place.

C) Obvious! No one around to see you, no one around who may have dropped it, may as well pick it up and keep it – finder's keepers!

3 **Your parents have asked you to help out with the gardening at the weekend ready for a family barbecue. What do you do?**

A) Your parents are always helping you out, so what's a couple of hours at the weekend? No big deal and they are your parents, after all.

B) You pledge them one hour on Saturday morning – you have made plans already and they wouldn't change their plans for you.

C) They must be having a laugh! The party will be full of olds and you really have got better things to do at the weekend. Why does a garden need to be tidy for a BBQ anyway?

Mainly As
You are clearly concerned about your relationship with others and your responsibility towards them. Kind, caring, considerate … are you sure you didn't cheat?!

Mainly Bs
Well, you seem a fairly well-balanced person, caring but also keenly aware of your own needs. Sometimes, however, you like to soothe your conscience by doing just enough good to get by – careful you don't fall into the dark side accidentally!!

Mainly Cs
Well, you clearly put yourself first, second and third in your life! Have you ever thought about other people's feelings before? You might want to be respected but that won't happen if you can't give out a little respect yourself.

Christians aim to be more like Christ each day they live. Clearly, they make mistakes but their intention is to do what is right and good, as they believe this is what God wants from them. For this reason, it is likely that in the quiz on page 82 Christians would want to fall into the 'a' category.

In order to know what to do in any given situation they are likely to rely on three things:

- the Bible
- their conscience
- FAITH in Christ.

The Bible

Christians often use the Bible to help them to make moral decisions (decisions about right and wrong). It contains advice in many different forms.

Specific commands

- The TEN COMMANDMENTS in Exodus 20 include the commandments to respect your parents, not to murder, and not to worship any IDOLS.
- In Matthew 22: 37–39 Jesus explains what the two greatest commandments are. The first is to love God with 'all your heart, soul and strength'. To love God completely in this way suggests that you will aim to please him in all you do. The second great commandment is to 'love your neighbour as yourself'. When Jesus refers to our neighbour in this passage he means anyone who needs our help, including those whom we may consider our enemies.

Parables

In the PARABLES Christians might find guidance on how they should behave. For example, the story of the Good Samaritan teaches people to care for everyone, even enemies.

General moral principles

These include ideas such as the principle that human life is SACRED.

The Bible does not contain examples of all the modern dilemmas that people might face. For example, it does not deal with abortion or euthanasia directly. However, Christians can study the general principles of behaviour that it contains and work out how to apply them to any decision that they have to make.

Many Christians work hard to identify the principles that should still apply to their behaviour today and those that are outdated and of less use. For example, many Christians disregard the teachings about what a woman should wear to church but place great importance on teachings about the value of human life.

Conscience

Christians believe that God has given people a sense of right and wrong. This is what is meant when they speak of their conscience. Christians believe that people can instinctively know whether what they are doing is right or wrong. If a person is doing wrong a Christian might say that the person will probably feel guilty or uneasy. In this way God is speaking to the person and helping them to recognise right from wrong.

God cannot force a person to take any notice of their conscience. It is possible to do something that is wrong and ignore any sense of guilt. In fact some people may even get to a point where they stop sensing right from wrong because they have ignored their conscience so often. Some Christians may ask God to help them sense right from wrong in a difficult decision, almost like asking for that sense to be made sharper. Other people might argue that a person's conscience is simply a result of the way that they have been brought up and has nothing to do with God.

Faith in Christ

Christians believe that Jesus came to earth and lived as a perfect man. They believe that all the decisions he made were the right ones and that he is an excellent example to follow in their own lives. Jesus exercised patience with people and went out of his way to help others, even those who weren't particularly nice to him or liked by society. Jesus spent time in PRAYER and asked God for guidance. He was always honest with people even though this upset them at times. He put people before money, land or possessions, and he was willing to make the ultimate SACRIFICE out of love for others by dying on the cross. Christians look at Jesus' lifestyle and attitudes and try to copy them in their own lives.

TASKS

Look at the bracelet in the photo. Some Christians choose to wear WWJD bracelets to help them continually to consider what Jesus would do if he were faced with the same daily decisions as them. Wearing a constant reminder of Jesus like this helps them to behave in a more Christ-like way on a daily basis.

1 Consider the three quiz questions on page 82. For each of them say what you think Jesus would do and why.

2 Jesus lived over 2000 years ago. How helpful do you think it is to ask the question 'What would he do?' in order to help you make a moral decision today?

The letters WWJD stand for What Would Jesus Do?

EXAM FOCUS ...

Explain how Christians might try to find the best way to behave.

question d), 6 marks

... HINTS

- This question is asking you to describe ways in which Christians can tell the difference between right and wrong but you also need to explain why these ways are good. So for instance, you might like to refer to the conscience. You would describe what this is and then explain that a Christian would listen to their conscience because to some it is the voice of God.

- You might like to refer to the way in which Jesus led his life and also of other famous Christians such as Martin Luther King Jr or Mother Teresa.

- You might like to refer to the Bible and then explain why following what is said in the Bible is important.

LET'S **RE**VISE

Different beliefs about God and the Devil

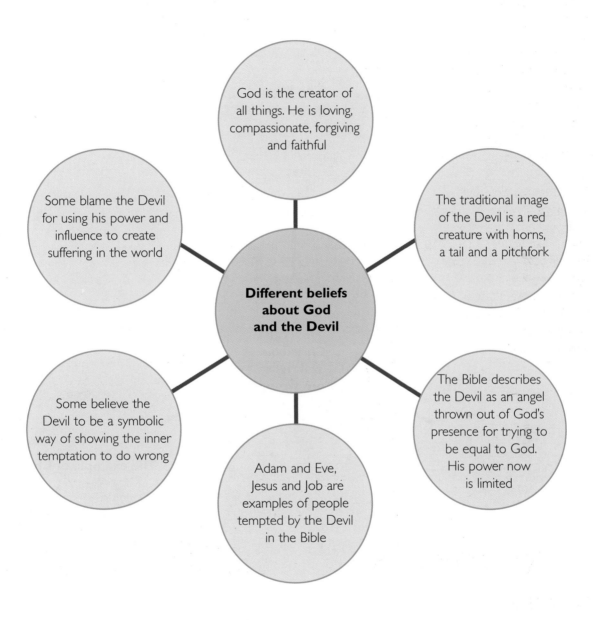

God is the creator of all things. He is loving, compassionate, forgiving and faithful

Some blame the Devil for using his power and influence to create suffering in the world

The traditional image of the Devil is a red creature with horns, a tail and a pitchfork

Different beliefs about God and the Devil

Some believe the Devil to be a symbolic way of showing the inner temptation to do wrong

The Bible describes the Devil as an angel thrown out of God's presence for trying to be equal to God. His power now is limited

Adam and Eve, Jesus and Job are examples of people tempted by the Devil in the Bible

TASK

Write a paragraph based on the diagram:

- Include each point and explain it clearly.

- Try to support each point with biblical references from your earlier work on this topic.

LET'S **RE**VISE

Sources and reasons for moral behaviour

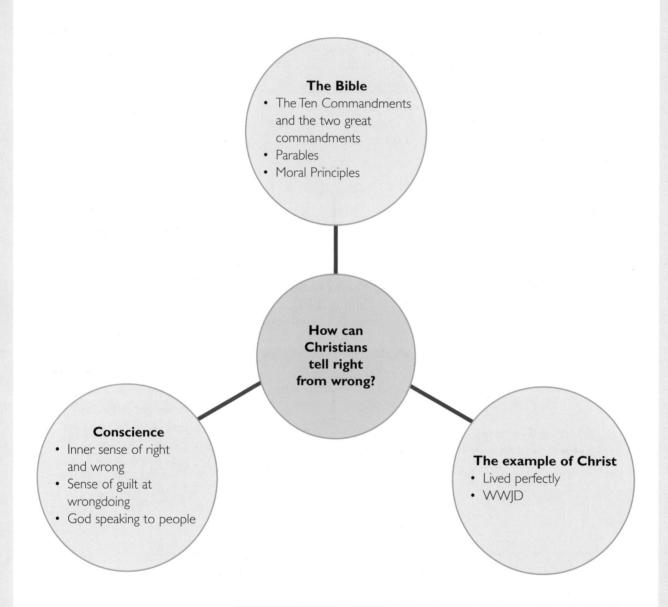

The Bible
- The Ten Commandments and the two great commandments
- Parables
- Moral Principles

How can Christians tell right from wrong?

Conscience
- Inner sense of right and wrong
- Sense of guilt at wrongdoing
- God speaking to people

The example of Christ
- Lived perfectly
- WWJD

TASKS

1 Write a paragraph on each of the three ways in which Christians can tell right from wrong.
2 Create revision cards of your own for the topic Good and Evil. Make sure you consider the following topics:

- Christian beliefs about good and evil.

- The problem of evil.

- Coping with suffering.

LET'S **RE**VISE

Exam focus

a) What is meant by redemption? *1 mark*

■ This question requires you to give a short description of what the word 'redemption' means. So you could say it is the act of saving someone from sin or saving someone from evil.

b) What is meant by the term 'original sin'? *2 marks*

■ This question is asking you to give two ideas about what happened when Adam and Eve disobeyed God in the Garden of Eden.

c) Describe Christian beliefs about God being good. *3 marks*

■ This question requires you to give three ideas on what God has done which Christians believe is good. So you might like to refer to the fact God performs miracles (giving examples) or that he came down in human form as Jesus to die on the cross so that believers can get to heaven (the atonement). You could support this latter idea with the quote from John 3: 16.

■ You might like to refer to God's commandments or teachings.

d) Explain how Christians respond to the idea that a loving God allows evil and suffering to exist in this world. *6 marks*

■ This question is asking you what Christians do or what they think about God not stopping bad things happening.

■ You might like to refer to practical ideas of what a Christian would do to help suffering people and link this to the idea that God expects people to show Christian love.

■ You might like to refer to the reasons Christians may give to explain why God does not intervene or even show that God does intervene on occasions and give examples.

e) 'Suffering is caused by the Devil.'
Discuss this statement. You should include different, supported points of view and a personal viewpoint. You must refer to Christianity in your answer. *12 marks*

■ Remember – it is important to show different points of view and also your own personal point of view.

■ This question is asking you to discuss and evaluate (look at the arguments for and against) and then come to a conclusion on whether the statement is true or false. You may not want to agree or disagree entirely – that is fine but you must support your conclusion with a valid reason.

■ You may like to refer to the traditional views of the devil and use these to show that Satan is the cause of suffering and link these to the example of Job.

■ You may like to refer to the idea of original sin and link this to the devil or to free will.

■ You may wish to refer to the devil as a symbol rather than a being who can interact in this world.

■ Remember to give your own personal view and support it.

Religion, Reason and Revelation

Key Concepts

In this topic you will learn about:

- Revelation through mystical and religious experience
- Revelation of God through the world
- Revelation of God in the person of Jesus
- The authority and importance of the Bible.

Christians believe that they are able to know God because he has chosen to reveal himself to human beings. Some Christians believe that they have had experiences of God where he has revealed himself to them personally, for example through visions. As creator, God is also believed to have revealed himself for all to see in the natural world. Although God the Father is himself invisible, Christians believe he revealed himself in the person of Jesus in order to meet directly with his people and to offer salvation through Jesus' death and RESURRECTION. God has also revealed himself through the Bible which has authority and importance for Christians as a SACRED text.

To discuss

1 What evidence is there in the account of Saul's conversion that suggests the experience was significant to him?

2 What explanation might a Christian give for why conversion may be accompanied by feelings of forgiveness, peace or joy?

TASKS

1 Read the Case Study on page 89 and describe the mystical experiences that St Teresa of Avila had.
2 What effect did these experiences have on her?
3 How does the imagery used by Ain Vares in the picture on page 89 opposite reflect the experience of Saul during his conversion?

Revelation through mystical and religious experience

When Christians speak about revelation they mean that God has disclosed something to humanity about himself. Christians believe that God's nature is revealed through the Bible, through the world and through his incarnation as Jesus.

Christians believe that Jesus came to earth in order to bring human beings closer to God. The Bible teaches that when a person becomes a Christian the Holy Spirit comes and lives within him or her. Some Christians experience God's presence within them in unexplainable ways which they feel gives them direct contact with God, for example through visions, an inner sense of his presence or baptism in the Holy Spirit. Experiences such as these are sometimes described as mystical or religious. Such experiences of God often come from a person meditating on him and his word, perhaps during times of personal PRAYER and CONTEMPLATION.

When a person becomes a Christian he or she may claim to have had a conversion experience. A person's conversion experience may include a complete sense of forgiveness, a sense of indescribable joy or the lifting of depression. For some Christians conversion is accompanied by a MIRACLE or the appearance of God in some visible form.

In the Bible, Saul, a man who was persecuting Christians, had a conversion experience. Saul was on his way to Damascus when a bright light from the sky blinded him, he fell to his knees and Jesus spoke to him, asking him why he was persecuting his followers. For three days Saul remained blind until Ananias was sent by God to place his hands on Saul's eyes, when Saul's sight was restored. Saul was immediately baptised, he began PREACHING in the synagogues that Jesus was Lord and Saul's name was changed to Paul.

Case study: St Teresa of Avila

St Teresa was born in Spain in 1515 and raised as a Christian. At 20 years of age she joined a convent outside Avila near Madrid in Spain. While there she became ill and early in her sickness she experienced times of what is called religious ecstasy. Religious ecstasy is described as an altered state of consciousness when the person has a great inner spiritual awareness, sometimes accompanied by visions of God. St Teresa became intensely aware of her own SIN and of ORIGINAL SIN and how awful this was to God. She realised that she needed to completely submit herself to the will of God. In 1559 she became certain that Jesus was present in her in bodily form although not visible. Her visions of Jesus in this way continued for two years. In another vision, a SERAPH drove the fiery point of a golden lance repeatedly through her heart, causing spiritual–bodily pain. In response to her mystical experiences she founded a new convent based on absolute poverty and went on to be an important reformer of the Roman Catholic order of nuns called the Carmelites.

Miracles

When God intervenes in the world and suspends the normal LAWS OF NATURE Christians would say that a miracle has occurred. Examples of miracles as recorded in the Bible would include the parting of the Red Sea by Moses, Jesus turning 180 gallons of water into wine and the paralysed being healed. Many Christians believe that God continues to act in miraculous ways today and that his presence can be experienced through them. The Catholic Church has verified 66 healing miracles at Lourdes over the past 150 years. Jesse Duplantis, an American pentecostal minister, claims that he has miraculously been taken into heaven itself and been visited by angels as a response to his prayers. Christians respond to these claims in diverse ways. Duplantis' ministry is well supported around the world, but other Christians are sceptical of his claims as they seem to contradict biblical teaching. For example, Jesse claims to comfort God and yet in the Bible God is the comforter of humans, he himself does not need comforting.

A Saviour is Born by the contemporary Estonian artist, Ain Vares.

EXAM FOCUS ...

Explain Christian beliefs about revelation.

question d), 6 marks

... HINTS

- You may like first to give examples of some of the ways in which Christians believe that God has revealed himself – in other words how he reveals himself. These examples could be: an answered prayer; the Bible; the person of Jesus; or a religious experience such as the experiences of Saint Teresa.
- You could then explain why these examples have such an impact on Christians; for example, you could relate the experiences of Saint Teresa to her founding the Carmelites.

Revelation of God through the world

Christians believe that the world reveals something about its creator. According to the Bible, God is the cause of the existence of the world, he is its designer and creator. This means Christians believe that without God there would be no world and no humanity. The world is grand and complex, it contains huge amounts of beauty and diversity. There is a natural order that ensures that in the food chain each species is provided for. Humans develop communities and each person has a conscience which helps us to identify right from wrong. Christians believe examples such as these reveal God's nature and reflect the teachings about God in the Bible, including his power, the order in his design, his father-like heart for people and his provision for all aspects of his creation.

Link it up

Look at the images of the world in the collage above. Divide a piece of paper into three columns as shown below.

1. For each image list the characteristics you think it reveals about God.
2. Compare these revelations with the Bible bitz on page 91 and match them up in the end column.
3. Write a paragraph to summarise what your table reveals to you about the character of God based on the natural world and the Bible quotes.

Image	Revelation about God	Bible Quote
B Waves crashing	Power and strength of God	Psalm 65: 7 Who stilled the roaring of the seas, the roaring of their waves

BB Bible bitz

You answer us with awesome deeds of righteousness,
O God our Saviour,
the hope of all the ends of the earth
and of the farthest seas,
who formed the mountains by your power,
having armed yourself with strength,
who stilled the roaring of the seas,
the roaring of their waves,
and the turmoil of the nations.

Psalm 65: 5–7

For since the creation of the world God's invisible qualities – his eternal power and divine nature – have been clearly seen, being understood from what has been made, so that men are without excuse.

Romans 1: 20

In the beginning, O Lord, you laid the foundations of the earth,
and the heavens are the work of your hands

Hebrews 1: 10

You alone are the Lord. You made the heavens, even the highest heavens, and all their starry host, the earth and all that is on it, the seas and all that is in them. You give life to everything, and the multitudes of heaven worship you.

Nehemiah 9: 6

This, then, is how you should pray: 'Our Father in heaven, hallowed be your name

Matthew 6: 9

Consider the ravens: They do not sow or reap, they have no storeroom or barn; yet God feeds them. And how much more valuable you are than birds!

Luke 12: 24

So God created man in his own image, in the image of God he created him; male and female he created them.

Genesis 1: 27

EXAM FOCUS ...

'God's power is revealed through nature.'

Discuss this statement. You should include different, supported points of view and a personal viewpoint. You must refer to Christianity in your answer.

question e), 12 marks

... HINTS

■ Remember – it is important to show different points of view and also your own personal point of view.
■ This question is asking you to discuss and evaluate (look at the arguments for and against) and then come to a conclusion about whether the statement is true or false. You may not want to agree or disagree entirely – this is fine but you must support your conclusion with a valid reason.
■ You could begin by agreeing with the statement and giving a Christian point of view that God reveals himself in many ways in the world and link this idea to a biblical quote (see the Bible bitz above).
■ You could disagree with the statement by stating that when natural disasters occur, such as tsunamis or earthquakes, if it is God's power then this raises the question why is God revealing himself in such a way.

Revelation of God in the person of Jesus

We are certain of the existence of many things in the world that are invisible to the human eye, for example, air, gravity and electricity. We can prove the existence of such things using visible examples. Look at the three pictures below and decide what invisible thing is suggested by visible evidence in each.

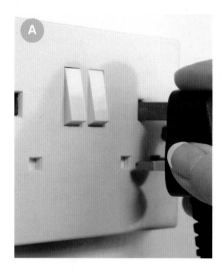

To discuss

Look at the cartoon and read its caption.

1   Why is the follower of Jesus in the cartoon shown to be opening a gift?

2   Why is the idea of finding eternal life in a gift wrapped box meant to be funny?

3   In what way does this idea link in with the statement in Colossians 1: 15 that says 'He is the image of the invisible God'.

ETERNAL LIFE, MY FAVORITE ... THANKS JESUS!

The Bible teaches that Jesus is the visible image of an invisible God (Colossians 1: 15). Christians believe that Jesus is the incarnation of God. Incarnation means God coming in the flesh. Through his life, teachings, MIRACLES, death and RESURRECTION Jesus revealed God more fully to humans. By entering the world in the form of a human God made himself more accessible to humans, as they are designed to relate to one another. By becoming human Christians believe that Jesus understood and shared in the human experience including joy, friendship and suffering. Christians believe that the incarnation showed that, although God is the great creator of the world, he is also willing to be humbled out of a love for the people he has created.

Bible bitz

Now this is eternal life: that they may know you, the only true God, and Jesus Christ, whom you have sent.

John 17: 3

I have come that they may have life, and have it to the full.

John 10: 10

For God did not send his Son into the world to condemn the world, but to save the world through him

John 3: 17

This is how God showed his love among us: He sent his one and only Son into the world that we might live through him

1 John 4: 9

Don't you believe that I am in the Father, and that the Father is in me? The words I say to you are not just my own. Rather, it is the Father, living in me, who is doing his work. Believe me when I say that I am in the Father and the Father is in me; or at least believe on the evidence of the miracles themselves. I tell you the truth, anyone who has faith in me will do what I have been doing. He will do even greater things than these, because I am going to the Father.

John 14: 10–12

STRETCH WHAT YOU KNOW

… that people often say about Him: 'I'm ready to accept Jesus as a great moral teacher, but I don't accept His claim to be God.' That is the one thing we must not say. A man who was merely a man and said the sort of things Jesus said would not be a great moral teacher. He would either be a lunatic – on a level with the man who says he is a poached egg – or else he would be the Devil of Hell. You must make your choice. Either this man was, and is, the Son of God: or else a madman or something worse. You can shut Him up for a fool, you can spit at Him and kill Him as a demon; or you can fall at His feet and call Him Lord and God. But let us not come with any patronising nonsense about His being a great human teacher. He has not left that open to us. He did not intend to.

Mere Christianity by C. S. Lewis

1 What claims do you think Jesus made that would lead people to consider him to be a lunatic?

2 What things did Jesus do that may lead some people to consider him to be a fool?

3 What reasons do Christians have for believing Jesus to be Lord?

4 Why do you think C. S. Lewis thought it was patronising to think of Jesus as a 'great human teacher'?

5 Explain what your own conclusion is about who Jesus was.

Link it up

Read the Bible bitz and use them to help you to answer these questions.

1 According to the Bible who caused Jesus to be in the world?

2 What reasons does Jesus give in these quotes for being in the world?

3 According to the Bible, what can humans learn and receive from Jesus' existence in the world?

EXAM FOCUS ...

Explain Christian beliefs about Jesus.

question d), 6 marks

... HINTS

■ To answer this you might like to begin by showing the reasons God appeared in human form and link them to one of the biblical quotes shown in the Bible bitz above.

■ You could show what Christians believe Jesus did while he was on earth such as his teachings and miracles but most importantly his death and resurrection.

The authority and importance of the Bible

A
You must teach your
children that the ground beneath
their feet is the ashes of our grandfathers.
So that they will respect the land, tell your
children that the earth is rich with the lives of our kin.
Teach your children that we have taught our children that
the earth is our mother. Whatever befalls the earth befalls
the sons of earth. If men spit upon the ground, they spit upon
themselves. This we know; the earth does not belong to man;
man belongs to the earth. This we know. All things are
connected like the blood which unites one family.

*Seattle, chief of the Suquamish
Indians (1786–1866)*

B
I have learned
that courage was not
the absence of fear, but
the triumph over it. The
brave man is not he who
does not feel afraid, but
he who conquers that fear.

*Nelson Mandela, first
democratically elected President
of South Africa, (1918–)*

C
Buddhists
should follow the
five precepts for
good behaviour: not to
harm any SENTIENT life,
not to steal, to live a pure
and restrained life, not to
lie or deceive, and not
to use INTOXICANTS.

*The Teaching of Buddha,
The Buddhist Bible*

To discuss

Read the quotes above. Each suggests an attitude towards life and offers some guidance on how a person should live.

1 What attitudes and guidelines does each quote give on living?

2 Who do you think is most likely to live by the ideas given in each quote?

3 Would you apply any of these attitudes and guidelines to your own life? Why?

We all seek to live by guidelines that are important to us. The source of these guidelines may be a person we greatly respect, like our parents, or a written source such as a holy book. These people or books may be said to have authority in our lives. For example, Buddhists would say that the teaching of the Buddha has authority over their lives, and so they will try not to kill any living creature according to the first precept. For this reason many Buddhists are vegetarians. For Christians, it is the Bible, the Word of God, which has authority in their lives.

Christian beliefs

For Christians the Bible is a SACRED test. This means it is holy as it is believed to be the revealed word of God. Christians believe that the Bible has authority in their lives. Christians interpret the Bible differently but they all believe that it is in some way the word of God.

Some Christians think that the Bible is without error because it is not the words of human beings but the exact words of God. These Christians believe that everything in the Bible is factually and literally (word for word) true. For example, they accept that the world was literally created in six days on God's spoken command. If science appears to contradict the Bible then the Bible is considered to be correct, since God does not make mistakes.

Other Christians believe that while the Bible is the word of God it has been written by humans, whose own personalities will have affected the content. These Christians believe that many truths about God can be discovered in the Bible but that it is not all meant to be taken literally. For example, when Jesus is said to have fed over 5000 people with just five loaves and two fish it is the example of sharing that is being taught. One boy gave his small lunch to Jesus, who shared it among his followers, and then others also began to share until all were fed. The MIRACLE is that people shared as a result of Jesus' example, not that the fish and loaves suddenly multiplied.

Another way Christians interpret the Bible is to think of the writers as having insights into God and life that they have been able to put into words. Some of the writers, such as Moses or Paul, might have had experiences of God that they have then tried to record. This way of interpreting the Bible acknowledges that it may contain mistakes. Often, parts of the Bible are understood as symbolic poetry and are not taken as factually true. For example, the idea that the world was created in six days is a way of showing that the world EVOLVED over a period of time.

However Christians interpret the Bible, they all believe it is holy and that God can speak to them through it. For this reason they seek to live in a way that is based on its teaching. The Bible offers Christians guidance on:

- how to worship God in a manner that is worthy
- how to treat others, whether friends or enemies
- the basic rules on which to base their lives
- moral behaviour
- spiritual support and encouragement in difficult times.

Mark

As a Christian I read the Bible every day for guidance in the way that I live my life. There are passages in the Bible that guide me in the choices that I make. For instance, Jesus gave moral direction and teaching in the PARABLES throughout the Gospels.

Reading the Bible develops my relationship with God as a Christian. David displayed faith and courage when he saved the Israelites from their enemies the Philistines. I exercise courage to a different degree by sharing my faith with others. I exercise faith in God when I struggle to find answers as problems in life come my way.

It is a tangible religious experience to receive God's comfort and peace by worshipping him when I don't feel like it. The Bible helps me to realise the Christian walk in life is measured by faith, not feelings.

The Bible teaches me that God's will for my life is to love him with my mind, body and soul. To develop human friendships requires consent and effort by the people involved. The same principle applies to me as I build a relationship with God. I believe that if I don't read my Bible daily then I miss out on learning a lesson that God has to teach me

The Bible meets people at whatever point they are in life. I believe that anyone who wants to can discover God's response to help them, whatever situation they are in.

TASKS

Read Mark's account on page 95.

1 Identify all the ways in which Mark says the Bible helps him in his life. Include any examples he gives to support what he is saying.

2 In what way does Mark say his relationship with God is like a human relationship?

3 Why does the Bible play an important part in developing his relationship with God?

4 Explain how you think the Bible is being used in each of the pictures A–D above. What does each tell you about the authority, significance and importance of the Bible for individuals, groups and society?

5 Why do you think Christians meet in small groups to study the Bible?

6 What benefit do you think Christians get from reading and meditating on the Bible on their own?

EXAM FOCUS ...

Explain how Christians may use the Bible in their lives.

question d), 6 marks

... HINTS

■ This question is asking you about the different ways a Christian uses the Bible *but* you will also need to state *why* they use the Bible and *why* it is important.

■ You could start by stating that the Bible is holy and that it is the 'word of God'.

■ You could then refer to the different ways a Christian might use the Bible and show why this use is important. For instance: you could say: 'If a Christian was upset because a loved one had died they might read the passage in the Bible which shows them God is with people in life and death' (Psalm 23).

LET'S **RE**VISE

Religion, Reason and Revelation

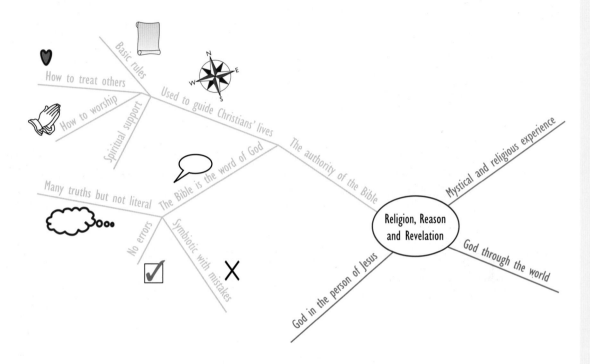

Mind maps are a way of revising that uses colour, picture and language, this makes it easier for the brain to recall the information.

When completing a mind map you need to follow a few simple rules to help make it effective:

- Each section must be completed in a separate colour.
- Each point must be written on a line of the same length.
- Each point needs a picture to go with it. Everyone's brain will link ideas to different images; the stranger or funnier you can make them the more effective they are for helping you to revise.
- You should use no more than three colours when doing the drawings on your mind map.

TASK

1 Copy out the mind map but create your own pictures for the yellow section.
2 Complete the other three sections of the mind map using your class work and the information in this chapter.
3 Attempt the exam focus questions from this chapter using only the mind map to trigger your memory.

LET'S REvise

Exam focus

a) What does the word 'mystical' mean?   *1 mark*

▓ Your answer should be a short explanation of the word 'mystical'. So you could state
that it refers to someone having a spiritual experience or experiencing an event which is
beyond human understanding.

b) What is meant by a religious experience?   *2 marks*

▓ You could briefly explain a religious experience in general terms or you could refer to
a specific event such as the conversion of St Paul or the experiences of Saint Teresa.

c) Describe how Christians believe God has revealed himself in the world.   *3 marks*

▓ You could give various examples of how God has shown himself such as:
the Bible as the revealed word of God; the person of Jesus; the world, etc.

d) Explain the importance of the revelation of God in the person of Jesus.   *6 marks*

▓ You might like to link the reasons why God came down in human form to biblical
teachings; for instance you could refer to the concept of Jesus as Saviour to the
biblical teaching of John 3: 17.

▓ You might like to link the work and teachings of Jesus to the concept of
Christians getting to heaven (John 14: 6).

e) 'The means of the teachings in the Bible have been changed so often that they are no longer true'.
Discuss this statement. You should include different, supported points of view
and a personal viewpoint. You must refer to Christianity in your answer.   *12 marks*

▓ Remember – it is important to show different points of view and also
your own personal point of view.

▓ This question is asking you to discuss and evaluate (look at the arguments for and against) and
then come to a conclusion on whether or not the statement is true or false. You may not want to
agree or disagree entirely – this is fine but you must support your conclusion with a valid reason.

▓ You may like to give the point of view of some Christians that the Bible is the
word of God and therefore every word is true regardless of time.

▓ You could counter-argue that the Bible was written over a long period of time and that
it has been translated many times and because humans can make mistakes then perhaps there
are some points which are not true, and perhaps support this idea with specific examples.

▓ You could give an atheist point of view.

▓ Remember to give your own supported conclusion.

LET'S **RE**VISE

Exam focus

a) What is meant by the word 'authority'.   *1 mark*

▓ This question is asking you to give a short explanation of what is meant by authority. You could state that it is the power to give orders, or if someone has authority you obey them.

b) Give two ways in which God has revealed himself.   *2 marks*

▓ This question is asking you for two ideas which Christians use to show God has intervened in this world. So you could use the Bible, the world, the person of Jesus or miracles.

c) Describe how Christians may use the Bible.   *3 marks*

▓ This question is asking you to give ways in which the Bible can be used and how it is important. So you could refer to the use of the Bible in church, the home or in a court.

d) Explain what Christians believe about religious experiences.   *6 marks*

▓ To begin your answer you would need to give a short description of what a religious experience is and then explain why this is important to Christians.

▓ You might like to use specific examples in your answer to show the importance of these events, such as the conversion of St Paul.

e) 'Sacred texts should be written in modern language so that everyone can understand them.' Discuss this statement. You should include different, supported points of view and a personal viewpoint. You must refer to Christianity in your answer.   *12 marks*

▓ Remember – it is important to show different points of view and also your own personal point of view.

▓ This question is asking you to discuss and evaluate (look at the arguments for and against) and then come to a conclusion on whether the statement is true or false. You may not want to agree or disagree entirely – that is fine but you must support your conclusion with a valid reason.

▓ You might like to refer to the different Christian interpretations of the Bible in your answer to either support or disagree with the statement.

▓ You might like to explain why it is important to understand the messages within the sacred text but at the same time why it would be wrong to corrupt that message.

▓ Remember to include your own personal view and support it.

Religion and Science

Key Concepts

In this topic you will learn about:

- Scientific theories about the origins of the world and humanity
- Christian teachings about the origins of the world and humanity
- The relationship between scientific and religious understandings of the origins of the world and humanity
- The place of humanity in relation to animals
- Attitudes to animals and their treatment
- Christian ideas about stewardship and their responses to environmental issues.

Christians' views on the origins of the universe and humanity vary. Some agree with modern scientific theories, whereas others take the biblical account of creation in Genesis literally, believing in six days of creation by God. Christians believe that God created humans to be different from other animals, by giving human beings the potential to have a relationship with him. All Christians believe that one of the roles that humans have been given on earth is that of STEWARDS, so they aim to care for the world around them and use its resources responsibly. For this reason Christians respond to environmental issues by trying to reduce the harm human behaviour may have on the world.

The question of how the world and humans originally came to exist is one that people have sought to answer for centuries. The study of the origins and nature of the universe is called COSMOLOGY. Aristotle (384–322BCE), a Greek PHILOSOPHER, taught that the universe had always existed and would always continue to exist. Whereas Augustine (354–430CE), a CHURCH FATHER, thought that the universe was created by God and was about 6000 years old. He based his teaching on his study of Genesis.

Many people today believe the universe was the result of a massive explosion between 14 billion and 19 billion years ago. However, some Christians believe the world is far younger. They accept the biblical account of creation that is given in Genesis. They believe the universe was created by God and that he created Adam and Eve as the first humans.

A cartoonist's impression of the creation of the world.

To discuss

Look at the cartoons on page 100 and on the right.

1 What view of the origins of the universe do you think each cartoon is supporting? How can you tell?

2 What do you currently believe about the origins of the universe? What reasons do you have for holding this view?

3 Do you think our significance as human beings is dependent on how the universe came into being?

A cartoonist's comment on the universe.

'We are just an advanced breed of monkeys on a minor planet of a very average star. But we can understand the universe. That makes us something very special.'

Stephen Hawking, scientist (1942–)

TASKS

Stephen Hawking is a British physicist. He is a professor at Cambridge University and is well known for his scientific contributions to cosmology.

1 Read Stephen Hawking's description of human beings on the left.

2 In pairs select one of the questions below and put together an answer to share with your class.

■ Do you agree with Stephen Hawking that the human race is no more than an advanced breed of monkeys?

■ Do you think Hawking's view leaves any room for the existence of a creator God?

Scientific theories about the origins of the world and humanity

Scientific knowledge is based on the development of theories. These theories are then tested through scientific experiments and observations in order to prove or disprove the original theory. A theory proven with enough scientific evidence provides us with factual knowledge about our world.

Scientists have developed theories about how the world began and how human beings originated. The most influential of the theories about the origins of the world is the Big Bang theory. EVOLUTION is the name given to the scientific theory for the origins of humanity.

'I think that it's important for scientists to explain their work, particularly in COSMOLOGY. This now answers many questions once asked of religion.'

Stephen Hawking, scientist (1942–)

To discuss

1 What reasons do you think Stephen Hawking has for suggesting that it is important for scientists to explain their work in cosmology?

2 What questions do you think people used to ask of religion that they now think have been answered by science?

The Big Bang theory

The Big Bang theory uses scientific evidence to suggest that the universe was formed as a result of a massive explosion, known as the Big Bang. From this explosion all the GALAXIES were formed as the universe expanded.

Scientists believe that several observations they have made about the universe today support the Big Bang theory. They have observed that:

■ the universe is still expanding, with galaxies moving further and further away from each other

■ the further away a galaxy is from our galaxy, the faster it moves.

In 1965 two scientists, Arno Allan Penzias and Robert Woodrow Wilson, discovered cosmic background radiation, which provides evidence of remnants of light from the very hot beginnings of the universe.

The observation that the universe is still expanding clearly suggests that in the past it must have been far smaller. In fact scientists consider that everything in the universe today was at one time concentrated in one single point. The heat Penzias and Wilson first observed also suggests that this single mass started expanding rapidly as a result of a hot explosion or big bang.

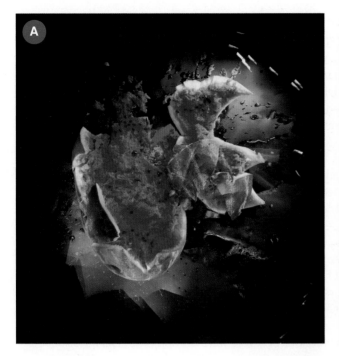

An exploding melon.

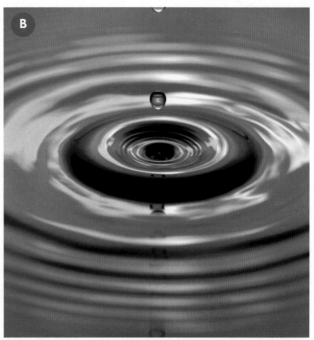

A ripple in water.

An exploding light bulb.

TASKS

Look at the images above and select one.

1 How does the image you have selected act as a helpful ANALOGY for the observations that scientists have made of our universe?

2 When considering the Big Bang theory, what are the limitations of the analogy that you have chosen?

STRETCH WHAT YOU KNOW

Go to www.bbc.co.uk/schools/gcsebitesize/science/aqa/radiation/originsrev1.shtml/.

Then select the section on the universe.

1 Read through the information about the universe, which gives more evidence about the Big Bang theory.

2 Complete Test Bite on the final page of the website.

3 How useful do you find this information in helping you to explain the origins of the universe?

Evolution

Charles Darwin (1809–82) was a scientist who explored the world on the ship HMS *Beagle*, and his discoveries are central to the theory of evolution. In 1859 he wrote *On the Origin of Species*. In this book he argued that life began with very simple cells and later developed into the different species we see today. He concluded from his studies that species gradually change and adapt to their environment, so the species best able to cope in a certain environmental condition will survive and reproduce, whereas the weaker species will die out. The next generation of the species will be slightly different, as it has adapted. As a result, over a long period of time, species change. Natural selection is the name he gave to the process by which the strongest animals and plants survive and the weakest die out.

Darwin concluded that his theory meant that human beings had also EVOLVED, and that in the past humans were not the same as we know them today. Darwin's theories suggested that humans share some of their ancestry with apes, and that human beings are a particularly well-adapted species of animal, not unique or set apart as religious believers would argue. This theory has received scientific support from the discovery of fossils from animals that are now extinct.

Obviously, many religious believers were unhappy with Darwin's findings. One scientist who was a Christian, a man named Phillip Gosse (1810–88), argued that the fossils had been put in the ground by God to test the FAITH of Christians.

TASKS

3 Draw your own cartoon **or** create a collage to show Darwin's ideas of evolution.

4 Do you think that there are any questions about the origins of the universe and humanity that science is not capable of answering? Explain your answer.

5 Do you think that a belief in a creator God is possible in the light of the scientific theories? Explain your answer.

When Darwin's ideas were first published, cartoons like this one were produced, which made fun of his theory that human beings had links with apes.

STRETCH WHAT YOU KNOW

4 Find out more about evolution and the ideas of Darwin by searching the BBC website, www.bbc.co.uk/darwin

5 Use this site or the information on this page to help you write an obituary for Darwin that focuses on his main scientific discoveries.

Christian teachings about the origins of the world and humanity

Christians believe that the reason the world exists is because God created it. The creation of the world by God was designed to perfectly suit the needs of human beings as well as all the other forms of life such as animals, fish and plants. According to the accounts in Genesis 1–3, when God speaks things come into existence. For example: 'God said, "Let there be light," and there was light' (Genesis 1: 2–4). Humans were created on the sixth day and are made like God, reflecting his nature and spiritual dimension; they are set apart from animals in this way and given authority over them.

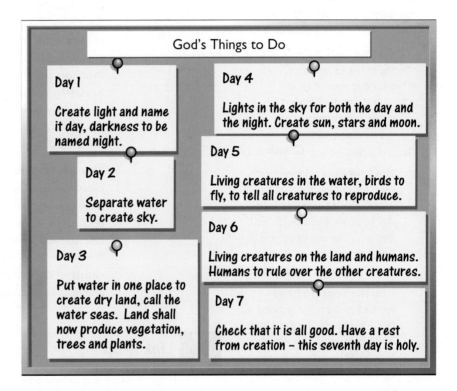

God's Things to Do

Day 1
Create light and name it day, darkness to be named night.

Day 2
Separate water to create sky.

Day 3
Put water in one place to create dry land, call the water seas. Land shall now produce vegetation, trees and plants.

Day 4
Lights in the sky for both the day and the night. Create sun, stars and moon.

Day 5
Living creatures in the water, birds to fly, to tell all creatures to reproduce.

Day 6
Living creatures on the land and humans. Humans to rule over the other creatures.

Day 7
Check that it is all good. Have a rest from creation – this seventh day is holy.

To discuss

1 Compare the order of God's things to do with what you understand from science about the development of the world. What things conflict?

2 If all creation was caused to exist simply through the commands of God what does this suggest about God's power and authority?

3 What possible reasons could the writer of Genesis have had for recording the creation story in this order?

BB Bible bitz

In the beginning God created the heavens and the earth. Now the earth was formless and empty, darkness was over the surface of the deep, and the Spirit of God was hovering over the waters. And God said, 'Let there be light', and there was light.

Genesis 1: 1–3

So God created man
    in his own image,
in the image of God
    he created him;
male and female
    he created them.

Genesis 1: 27

The Lord God formed the man from the dust of the ground and breathed into his nostrils the breath of life, and the man became a living being.

Genesis 2: 7

Now the Lord God had formed out of the ground all the beasts of the field and all the birds of the air. He brought them to the man to see what he would name them.

Genesis 2: 19

The earth is the Lord's, and everything in it, the world, and all who live in it.

Psalm 24: 1

Clare

How do I think the earth and us humans came to be here? I don't buy into this Big Bang theory. How can something so amazingly awesome as this world be a result of a scientific mishap? What about this idea that we come from a long line of apes, too? I've seen some people behaving like animals and occasionally looking pretty rough, but who really could believe this concept?

I understand that things evolve over time; you only have to look at the humble wireless radio and how that has changed in a matter of a few years to the MP3 players to see that technology is continually pushing the boundaries forward. But how does that work for us humans? Did we honestly just start out as animals and progress to where we are now simply over time? This idea isn't one that I think stacks up. Some being, some higher power had to have a hand in this.

This world that we inhabit could only be the creation of a mastermind, a genius architect, a true MIRACLE worker, one God. At least that is my opinion and many other people besides. As a Christian I believe in the creation story, that the earth and those that live within it are a result of God's perfect planning and not of some chaotic catastrophe.

Link it up

1 Clare says she believes that the origins of the universe and humanity are the result of God's perfect planning. Think about the order in which events take place in the creation story and the Bible quotes. What details from these accounts could be used to support this belief?

2 Do you think it is necessary to accept the Genesis account literally in order to believe, like Clare does, that the master mind of God was behind the origins of the universe? Explain your answer.

EXAM FOCUS …

Explain Christian attitudes to the origins of the world and humanity.

question d), 6 marks

… HINTS

■ The keyword in this question is 'attitudes' so this means you have to address the different Christian beliefs about the biblical teachings of how the world was created and how God made human beings.

■ You may like to begin with the attitude that Genesis 1 and Genesis 2 are the true word of God. Remember to say how both the world and humans were created.

■ You could then refer to the idea that some Christians believe that Genesis 1 and 2 are stories which symbolically show God's power and that the accounts are there to show why God created the world rather than how.

The relationship between scientific and religious understandings of the origins of the world and humanity

The Genesis accounts of the origins of the world rely on the existence of God. Creation takes place over what is described as six days. In the creation story God speaks and the universe forms from nothing. Everything that is formed is described as good. Nothing in this account of the creation happens by chance and everything that God makes has a purpose or reason for being. Genesis makes no mention of a Big Bang or of EVOLUTION over billions of years. In this way, the biblical account appears to contradict science.

Some Christians take the account in Genesis literally, believing the conclusions of science to be mistaken. These Christians believe that it is important not to take parts of the Bible and to accept them as myth or symbolic stories, because this would undermine the core beliefs that they hold. God has spoken directly and clearly to humans through his written word, the Bible, and it is through FAITH that people should accept the truth that it contains.

Many Christians, however, believe that science has correctly observed how the universe originated, and that the Bible provides a symbolic expression of the development of the universe. In this case the days spoken of in the Genesis account might be recognised as simply representing periods of time over which the developments occurred, in line with scientific beliefs about the evolutionary process. The Genesis account is not viewed as a historical account but rather as an account that gives purpose and direction to the world – a world in which God is involved and for which he is to be PRAISED. These Christians might also argue that Genesis was not written to explain how the universe came into existence, but rather to answer questions of meaning, such as 'Do humans have a purpose?'

TASKS

1 Explain what God is meant to be doing in William Blake's painting.
2 What Christian beliefs about the existence of the world does the painting reinforce? For example, it is planned and designed?
3 Draw a picture or create a collage to illustrate your own view of the origins of the world and humanity.

The Ancient of Days by William Blake (1757–1827), 1794.

STRETCH WHAT YOU KNOW

John Polkinghorne (left) is an internationally recognised scientist, author and vicar. He thinks that science and Christianity do not conflict. Below is an extract from a radio interview that he gave in 2002.

> When physicists study the world they are very struck by the beautiful order of the world, and the fruitful history of the world. The universe started about 15 billion years ago just as a ball of energy; now it is very rich and differentiated, it has human beings and all sorts of remarkable consequences of its history. That does suggest that there is rather more to tell about the intelligibility of the world … than science on its own is able to articulate and express … I believe the order of the world is an expression of the mind of the creator, the fruitfulness of the world is an expression of the creator's purpose … it is not an accident … I don't say to my atheist friend that you are stupid if you don't see it this way but I do say to them, look, it's not just a happy accident, there is a meaning and a purpose behind it all.

1 John Polkinghorne speaks about the order of the world being an expression of the creator's mind. In what ways can order be observed in our world?

2 If the fruitfulness of the world is an expression of the creator's purpose, explain what this means.

3 Do you think that it is necessary for there to be a creator in order for you to have a purpose in life?

You can listen to other parts of this interview by logging on to: www.counterbalance.net/transcript/ssq2-body.html

EXAM FOCUS …

Explain why Christian beliefs about the origins of the universe and humanity are different to scientific theories.

question d), 6 marks

… HINTS

■ This question is asking you to explain why some Christian beliefs about how the universe began are different to scientific ones, so make sure you show how and why the ideas are different.

■ You could refer to the different Christian interpretations of the two creation accounts in Genesis and how the literal view shows that God created the universe and not the Big Bang, but the symbolic account shows Christians why God created the universe while science explains how it was created.

■ You could refer to the view that some Christians believe God was responsible for the Big Bang and so although they agree that the universe began with the Big Bang they do not agree with the fact that it happened by random chance.

■ You could refer to the fact that Christians believe that humans were created by God in a special way 'in his image' (Genesis 1: 27) whereas scientists believe in Darwin's theory of evolution and survival of the fittest.

The place of humanity in relation to animals

Bible bitz

Do not be afraid of those who kill the body but cannot kill the soul.

Matthew 10: 28

Do you not know that your body is a temple of the Holy Spirit, who is in you, whom you have received from God?

1 Corinthians 6: 19

For God so loved the world that he gave his one and only Son, that whoever believes in him shall not perish but have eternal life.

John 3: 16

For great is your [God's] love, reaching to the heavens.

Psalm 57: 10

Christ Jesus might display his unlimited patience as an example for those who would believe in him.

1 Timothy 1: 16

You are forgiving and good, O Lord.

Psalm 86: 5

I will ascribe justice to my Maker.

Job 36: 3

According to Genesis 1: 27, humans, unlike animals, were created in the image of God. Christians do not think that humans have a physical likeness to God but rather that humans possess something of the nature (characteristics) of God.

Many Christians also believe that humans, unlike animals, have a soul that is ETERNAL (Matthew 10: 28). This means that after physical death the soul of a human being will continue to live on. Christians believe that human beings have been created to PRAISE and serve God and to enjoy God's company forever. They believe human life is special and unique. In John 3: 16, it says that God loved humanity so much he was willing to allow his son to die in order to restore a relationship with human beings, a relationship that had been broken through human disobedience. The Bible does not speak of any other created being as having the potential to have a relationship with God.

Humans have rights and duties that are not shared with any other creature. A good example of human duties towards God and one another is the list of the TEN COMMANDMENTS in Exodus 20, which includes the commandments to love and worship God, not to steal and not to murder. An example of one of the rights given to humans is the right to rule over the world God has created. This includes having authority over animals (Genesis 1: 28, see page 115).

For these reasons many Christians believe that there is a definite distinction between humans and animals.

The 12-year-old executioner
Daily Mail, online news, 25 April 2007

Police arrest six in anti-terror raids
Daily Telegraph, 24 April 2007

College ignored warnings about killer
Daily Telegraph, 18 April 2007

British battle tank damaged by Iraq bomb
Daily Telegraph, 23 April 2007

Journalist's parents plead: Is our kidnap son still alive?
Daily Telegraph, 16 April 2007

Link it up

1 From reading the Bible quotes above, can you identify some characteristics of God that you think you can also identify in humanity?

2 Explain what Christians mean when they say that they believe humans were created in the image of God.

TASKS

1 Look at the newspaper headings above.

  ▪ In pairs or small groups draw the outline of a human head and within it write words that describe the type of humanity portrayed through the newspaper headlines.

  ▪ Compare this to the characteristics of God that you identified in question 1 of the Link it up task. What are the differences between the two descriptions?

  ▪ Why do you think there are differences? What conclusions might you come to as a result of thinking about these differences?

2 Read Genesis chapter 3 in the Bible. Based on this account, what reason might a Christian give for the failure of humans to reflect the image of God in their lives?

The seventh day is a Sabbath to the Lord your God. On it you shall not do any work, neither you, nor your son or daughter, nor your manservant or maidservant, nor your ox, your donkey or any of your animals, nor the alien within your gates, so that your manservant and maidservant may rest, as you do.

Deuteronomy 5: 13–15

The Lord God made garments of skin for Adam and his wife and clothed them.

Genesis 3: 21

Everything that lives and moves will be food for you. Just as I gave you the green plants, I now give you everything.

Genesis 9: 1

Then God said, 'Let us make man in our image, in our likeness, and let them rule over the fish of the sea and the birds of the air, over the livestock, over all the earth, and over all the creatures that move along the ground.'

Genesis 1: 26

Consider the ravens: They do not sow or reap, they have no storeroom or barn; yet God feeds them. And how much more valuable you are than birds!

Luke 12: 24

Attitudes to animals and their treatment

Christians believe that as rulers over animals it is acceptable to use animals for human benefit. However, humans also have a responsibility to ensure that animals are cared for and kept in acceptable conditions and are not abused or mistreated. This is because they believe everything in the world belongs to God (Psalm 24 on page 106). Unnecessary or abusive use of animals goes against this teaching. For this reason many Christians disagree with the use of animals for cosmetics testing or for non-essential clothing such as produced by the fur trade.

All Church teachings reflect the concern for the environment and the care of animals that is called for in the Bible. Both the Catholic Church and the Church of England offer specific teachings on the use of animals in relation to medical research.

The Catholic Church

The Catholic Church states that 'medical and scientific experimentation on animals is a morally acceptable practice if it remains within reasonable limits and contributes to caring for or saving human lives'. However, the Church also teaches that unnecessary suffering should never be inflicted on animals.

The Church of England

In a similar fashion, the Church of England also teaches that humans have a responsibility to care for the welfare of animals, even though it may be necessary at times to use them in experiments, for example in initial medical research into a new drug or disease. When animals are used in medical experimentation the Church believes that any suffering needs to be kept to a minimum.

Link it up

Read the Bible quotes and answer the following questions.

1. In the Bible, to whom does God give authority over animals?

2. How does God expect humans to treat animals?

3. In what ways do the Bible quotes suggest it is acceptable to use animals?

4. Can you give some modern examples of the way in which the Bible says animals can be used? For example, a modern use of animals for work would be police or fire dogs.

5. Do you consider any use of animals to be unacceptable? Explain your answer.

To discuss

1. Read the 'In the News' article on page 111. What work were the navy dolphins trained to do?

2. Explain what response a Christian may have to the use of any animals in this way. Refer to the Bible bitz to help you in your answer.

3. Do you think it is acceptable to train animals to work in this way for humans?

Iranians buy Soviet 'killer' dolphins

The Times, by Richard Beeston, 10 March 2000

A squad of former Soviet Navy dolphins, trained to kill enemy divers and blow up ships, have become the world's first 'animal mercenaries', after they were sold to Iran by the Crimean authorities, who could not afford to keep them.

In what must rank as one of the most bizarre sell-offs of the post-Cold War Soviet arsenal, 27 naval amphibians, including dolphins, Beluga whales, walruses and sea lions, were transported by air to an undisclosed Iranian base on the Gulf.

Although dolphins have a popular image as clever and friendly, during the Cold War both the US and the Soviet Union developed secret training schools where the animals became skilled in detecting mines and carrying explosive charges which would explode on contact with enemy ships.

The newly imported dolphins from the former Soviet Navy's Black Sea Fleet headquarters in Sevastopol will not be the first naval dolphins to go into action in the region. The US Navy deployed five dolphins in the Gulf in 1987 to protect its warships from Iranian mines.

EXAM FOCUS ...

1 'Humans are nothing more than animals.'

Discuss this statement. You should include different, supported points of view and a personal viewpoint. You must refer to Christianity in your answer.

question e), 12 marks

2 Describe Christian attitudes to the treatment of animals.

question d), 6 marks

... HINTS

Question 1
■ Remember – it is important to show different points of view and also your own personal point of view.
■ This question is asking you to discuss and evaluate (look at the arguments for and against) and then come to a conclusion on whether the statement is true or false. You may not want to agree or disagree entirely – that is fine but you must support your conclusion with a valid reason.
■ You may like to refer to the fact that some Christians believe that humans are more important, as a way of disagreeing with the statement, because they were made for a special purpose by God and were given a soul, and then contrast this to the Quaker idea that all of God's creations are equally important.
■ You could refer to the scientific view of evolution to agree with the statement.
■ You could refer to human behaviour and how at times it looks as though animals are better behaved.
■ Remember to include your own viewpoint.

Question 2
■ The keyword in this question is 'attitudes' so this means that Christians have different ideas on how animals should be treated.
■ You may like to show the idea that animals and humans are all God's creation and therefore they should be treated equally – no medical testing on animals for instance. This idea relates to stewardship.
■ You might then like to note that some Christians believe in 'dominion' (Genesis 1: 28) and feel that humans are more important than animals and so therefore they can use animals for medical testing to help save the lives of humans.
■ You might like to refer to the idea that the use of animals in medical testing (not for beauty products) is seen as the 'lesser of two evils' but that it can only be done if the animals are treated in a good way.

Christian ideas about stewardship and their responses to environmental issues

Christians believe that the earth and all that is on it belong to God. However, he has given people the role on earth of stewards. This means acting as caretakers for both the earth and its inhabitants.

Overusing natural resources or destroying habitats is unacceptable to Christians. It is an abuse of God's trust. In practical terms being a steward should mean that human beings protect the environment and animals from EXPLOITATION, by caring for the world that they are part of and preserving it for future generations.

Christians can act as good stewards in their everyday lives by:

■ recycling as much of their waste as possible

■ choosing carefully the products that they consume – for example, by buying Fairtrade products and buying only as much as they really need

■ using efficient and eco-friendly energy sources in their homes, such as solar panels to generate electricity.

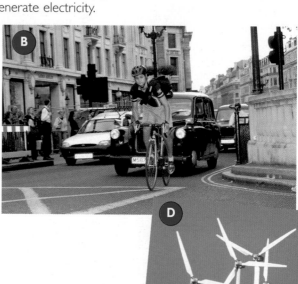

To discuss

1 Which environmentally friendly action do you think is being suggested by each of the images A–E on this page?

2 How many of these actions do you do regularly? Why?

3 Do you think it is important for people to think about their impact on the environment and try to protect it? Why?

Christians might also get involved in conservation groups or environmental campaigns. Two of the most well-known groups are Greenpeace and Friends of the Earth. Neither of these charities was set up because of a Christian concept of stewardship, but they both reflect the Christian ideals of caring for the environment and acting as good stewards. There are other charities and organisations that are based on Christian beliefs. These include A Rocha and The European Christian Environmental Network.

Case Study: A Rocha

A Rocha, meaning The Rock, is a Christian nature conservation organisation. It aims to show God's love for creation primarily through practical projects and environmental education. It was started in 1983 in Portugal by Peter and Miranda Harris and now works in over 15 countries across five continents.

A Rocha's first UK project was launched in 2001 and is called Living Waterways. It is based in west London in a heavily built-up and culturally diverse area. A Rocha Living Waterways has been working with the local council and community to turn a 90-acre wasteland site into a country park with recreational space and nature conservation areas. The project is also working to help local young people to appreciate and understand the natural environment around them.

Environment Sunday

A Rocha has promoted Environment Sunday for over eight years. It is an opportunity for churches to focus on:

- biblical teaching on God's world and humans' place in it
- Christian perspectives on the issue of the environment
- making a practical difference in their local community.

A Rocha provides support packs for churches to help them put together special services for this day. It is a time to focus on God's earth and humans' responsibility for it.

People can get involved with the work of the charity by donating money, volunteering to help – with fundraising, administration or projects in the community – and by supporting Environment Sunday.

How the area used to look before A Rocha began work.

How the area looks today.

STRETCH WHAT YOU KNOW

1 Visit the A Rocha International website at www.arocha.org and find out what work they are currently doing in two of the following places:

- Brazil
- Finland
- Lebanon
- USA
- Peru.

2 Write a report of A Rocha's work that could be used in a school magazine.

Church action

Christians can take individual action to care for the environment but they can also be good stewards by working as a community through their churches. The *Church Times*, a Christian newspaper, runs the national Green Church award. The Green Church website (www.greenchurchawards.org) describes the aims of the award as:

- to acknowledge, encourage and support the practical environmental work done by churches and their CONGREGATIONS

- to spread the word about environmental action and encourage other congregations to get started

- to celebrate good practice, by featuring the shortlisted projects in the *Church Times* and at an awards ceremony.

To discuss

4 Do you think that having a Green Church award is a good idea?

5 How might this award benefit the communities with which each church is involved?

6 Churches should be as green as possible in order to fulfil the role of stewards that God has given to human beings. The winning church in the competition is rewarded with a church makeover to make it more environmentally friendly. This prize is worth up to £3000. Do you think this is appropriate?

the *Church Times*
Green Church Awards

This is an innovative set of awards to celebrate what churches and individuals have done to help make the planet a place of safety and justice.

Key players in the Christian movement for environmental sustainability have come together to create and judge the awards, which aim to highlight the outstanding work being done by many churches in the UK. There is plenty more to do, of course, but, by telling some of the stories of existing projects, we hope to inspire others to follow their example.

The awards and their sponsors:

Action with the community
Conservation Foundation
Biodiversity
A Rocha UK
Campaigning to cut the carbon
Operation Noah/Christian Ecology Link
Celebrating creation
Eco-congregation
Changing lifestyles
Tearfund/ A Rocha's Living Lightly 24:1
Energy-saving in church buildings
Shrinking the Footprint/Marches Energy Agency
International action
Christian Aid
Young people
Christian Aid
Overall award:
best of the best
Church Times

Details and application forms can be found on www.greenchurchawards.org. The deadline for applications is 30 June. We will publish details of the shortlisted entries in the summer, and there will be an award ceremony in the autumn.

www.greenchurchawards.org

A poster advertising the Green Church awards.

Link it up

Using the Bible quotes on the right explain why Christians believe that they have a duty to care for the earth and its inhabitants.

Bible bitz

Then God said, 'Let us make man in our image, in our likeness, and let them rule over the fish of the sea and the birds of the air, over the livestock, over all the earth, and over all creatures that move along the ground.'

Genesis 1: 26

The earth is the Lord's, and everything in it, the world and all who live in it.

Psalm 24: 1

Every animal of the forest is mine,
and the cattle on a thousand hills.
I know every bird in the mountains,
And the creatures of the field are mine.

Psalm 50: 10–11

EXAM FOCUS ...

Explain how and why a Christian might act as a steward.

question d), 6 marks

God blessed them and said to them, 'Be fruitful and increase in number; fill the earth and subdue it. Rule over the fish of the sea, the birds of the air and over every living creature that moves along the ground.'

Genesis 1: 28

God saw all that he had made, and it was very good.

Genesis 1: 31

... HINTS

- This question is in two parts so make sure you answer both parts. You might like to begin by giving a brief explanation as to what a steward is.
- You could then give examples of how a Christian might show care for the world and link up these actions to a Christian teaching on caring for the world. For instance, you could state that a Christian might join an environmental protection group such as Greenpeace because in Genesis 2: 6–7 it tells of how God made Adam to 'work the ground'.

- You could refer to the fact the world belongs to God because he created it, and thus a Christian might protest about deforestation because of what is said in Psalm 24: 1.
- You could refer to the fact that if we misuse the world today there will be nothing left for future generations and thus Christians would not be obeying the commandment to 'love thy neighbour'.

Religion and Science

LET'S **RE**VISE

Scientific theories about the origins of the world and humanity

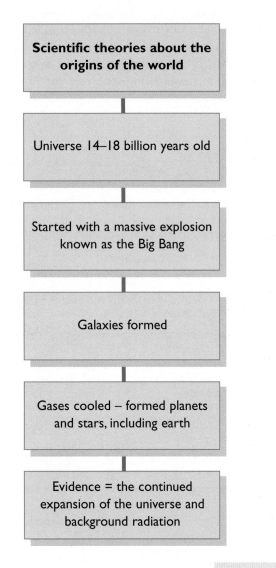

Scientific theories about the origins of the world

↓

Universe 14–18 billion years old

↓

Started with a massive explosion known as the Big Bang

↓

Galaxies formed

↓

Gases cooled – formed planets and stars, including earth

↓

Evidence = the continued expansion of the universe and background radiation

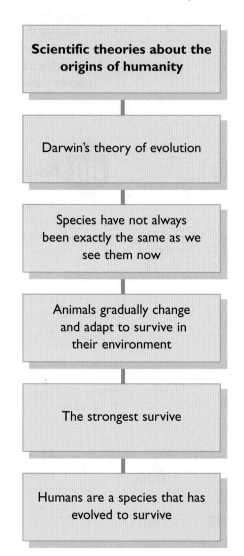

Scientific theories about the origins of humanity

↓

Darwin's theory of evolution

↓

Species have not always been exactly the same as we see them now

↓

Animals gradually change and adapt to survive in their environment

↓

The strongest survive

↓

Humans are a species that has evolved to survive

TASKS

1 Photocopy and cut out each of the information boxes in this diagram, then shuffle all the pieces. With a partner, remake the diagram, placing each box in the correct position.

2 Write two paragraphs explaining the scientific theories about the origins of the universe and humanity.

3 Create revision cards of your own for the topic Religion and Science. For example on:

■ Christian teachings about the origins of the world and humanity

■ The place of humanity in relation to animals

■ Christian ideas about stewardship.

LET'S **RE**VISE

Exam focus

a) What is meant by the term 'Big Bang'?   *1 mark*

■ The question is asking you to give a short explanation of the Big Bang. So you could say 'it is how science believes the world began' or 'the explosion which started off the world or universe'.

b) How does science believe humans began?   *2 marks*

■ For this answer you will need to give two ideas to answer the question because you will receive one mark per idea. So, you could refer to Darwin and his theory of the survival of the fittest through evolution. You could refer to humans evolving from the primordial slime and changing and adapting until humans evolved from monkeys.

c) Why do some Christians believe that animals are different to human beings?   *3 marks*

■ You could mention that some Christians believe animals do not have souls and support this with reference to how Adam was created. Or you could say that humans were made last in Genesis 1 and so this makes them more important. Or you could refer to the idea that Adam named all the animals (Genesis 2) which showed he was more important.

■ Or you could refer to the idea of 'dominion' and support this with the quote 'rule over' (Genesis 1: 28).

d) Explain why Christians believe it is important to look after the environment.   *6 marks*

■ The question is asking you 'why' not 'how' so do not fall into the trap of explaining what a Christian would do as a steward.

■ You could refer to the fact that God created the world and gave humans the responsibility of stewardship and support this with the idea that Adam was made to look after the Garden of Eden (Genesis 2).

■ There are also other biblical teachings from the Old Testament (Deuteronomy 24: 19 and 25: 4).

■ You could refer to Church teachings/instructions on helping the environment.

e) 'Science is right about how the world began and so religion is wrong.'
Discuss this statement. You should include different, supported points of view and
a personal viewpoint. You must refer to Christianity in your answer.   *12 marks*

■ Remember – it is important to show different points of view and also your own personal point of view.

■ This question is asking you to discuss and evaluate (look at the arguments for and against) and then come to a conclusion on whether the statement is true or false. You may not want to agree or disagree entirely – that is fine but you must support your conclusion with a valid reason.

■ You could start your answer by stating the difference between the scientific view and the Christian ideas on how the world began. Then you would need to support these ideas with 'evidence' and discuss whether or not either view has the definitive answer. You could refer to the fact that some scientists are Christians and therefore they believe that science explains the 'how' whilst religion explains the 'why'.

■ Remember to give your own point of view and support it.

Glossary

Abdicate   to give up power or responsibility

Adoration   worship

Allude   to refer to

Amen   meaning 'so let it be'

Analogy   a comparison; a similarity

Anglicans   members of the Church of England

Apostles' Creed   a statement of beliefs based on the teaching of the founders of Christianity

Ascension   Jesus' return to heaven after his resurrection

Atoning   making amends for; restoring a relationship

Baptismal pool   a pool in which people are baptised by being fully immersed in water

Church Fathers   founders of the Church

Committal statement   words used at the graveside as the body is lowered into the ground or at the crematorium as the coffin is taken out for cremation

Communal   shared; belonging to a community or group

Compassion   a sense of sympathy for others and a desire to help them

Confession   confessing sins directly to God, or possibly to a priest, asking for forgiveness

Congregation   a group of people gathered together for worship

Contemplation   quiet thought; meditation

Cosmology   the study of the origins of the universe

Cosmos   a universe that is ordered and harmonious

Covenant   a promise

Cremation   the burning of a corpse

Crucifix   an image of Christ on the cross

Doctrine   a specific teaching

Epitaph   short phrase or poem traditionally inscribed on to a headstone

Essence   in philosophy, an object's essence is what makes the object what it is

Eternal   without a beginning or an end

Eulogy   the speech given at a funeral about the dead person

Evolution   the process by which living things change and develop over a very long period

Evolve   to develop through a natural process

Exploitation   taking advantage of

Faith   belief without proof

Fall   term used to refer to Adam and Eve's disobedience to God, through which humankind lost its state of innocence and sin entered the world

Fasting   going without food and or drink

Galaxy   a cluster of billions of stars held together by gravity

Gospel   meaning 'good news', it refers to the first four books of the New Testament

Hallowed   holy

Holy Communion   the service during which bread and wine are shared in remembrance of the death and resurrection of Jesus

Idol   an image that is worshipped

Immortal   never to die

Incarnated   in human flesh; for example God appearing on earth in the physical body of Jesus

Infer   to draw a conclusion from

Intoxicants   a substance such as alcohol that produces feelings of pleasure or happiness

Kneelers   cushions that people kneel on to pray

Laws of nature   the rules that govern the natural world

Liturgical   relating to an order of service with set words and actions

Liturgical year   the Christian year which is made up of the cycle of worship in Christian Churches which determines when celebrations are, such as Easter.

Mass   the name used for Holy Communion (or the Eucharist) in the Roman Catholic Church

Material   physical matter

Miracle   a supernatural event or act

Mutability   capacity to change

Original sin   human sin that Christians believe is in every human being as a result of the Fall

Orthodox   belonging to the Eastern branch of the Christian Church

Parable   a story that illustrates a moral or religious meaning

Paschal candle   a large, white candle that is blessed and lit every year at Easter, and is used throughout the season of Easter and then throughout the year on special occasions, such as baptisms and funerals

Pentecost   the coming of the Holy Spirit to believers 50 days after the resurrection of Christ

Philosophers   thinkers

Pilgrims   people undertaking a journey to a place of religious importance for a spiritual reason

Praise   to give glory to

Prayers   words or thoughts addressed to God, requesting help, asking forgiveness or giving thanks

Preaching   giving a sermon; telling a group of people about God

Purification   the process of making something or someone clean; it often has the meaning of making someone clean of sin

Repentant   feeling sorry for something you have done, with a desire to change

Resurrection   being raised from the dead to new life

Sacrament   a Christian ceremony, such as baptism and Holy Communion, through which believers enter into a special relationship with God

Sacred   regarded as holy

Sacrifice   something that is offered up or given up; it often means something that is offered to God

Sentient   aware; able to respond to the senses

Seraph   an angel

Sermon   a religious talk, often with a moral theme

Sin   an act of disobedience against the rules of God

Speak in tongues   when a person speaks in a language not known to them, believed to be an ability given to them by God

Stations of the Cross   a series of images that represent stages on Jesus' last journey to his crucifixion; they are often found in churches and provide a focus for prayer and meditation

Steward   someone who takes responsibility for the care of a property; in Christian terms means taking responsibility for the care of God's creation

Supernatural   beyond the powers or laws of nature

Supremacy   supreme power or authority

Supplication   a request

Symbol   a sign, shape or object that is used to represent something else

Ten Commandments   laws believed to have been given by God to Moses

Transubstantiation   the conversion of bread and wine used in Holy Communion into the body and blood of Christ

Trinity   the three persons of God in one

Answers to task 1 on pages 74–75

A – molten lava from a volcano in Hawaii burning trees

B – destruction caused by the Boxing Day Tsunami, 2004

C – British casualties being evacuated from Iraq in the second Gulf War, 25 March 2003

D – rescue workers in Indonesia after an earthquake, 6 March 2007

E – fatal crash on the M40 in Buckinghamshire, Britain, 31 May 2007

F – the attack on the World Trade Center, New York, 11 September 2001

Index